The Book of Real
Missouri Records

Ross Malone

Back Cover:

Pictured on the back cover of this book is one of the many record holding teams with which you might not be familiar. This is the 1914 football team from the Missouri School of Mines at Rolla. (Now known as the Missouri University of Science and Technology.) This is considered to be the best college football team that ever played the game! Read more about them in the "Missouri's Best Sports" section.

My grandson, Conor, gave me the idea for this book. He is curious about what is the biggest, fastest, and best of everything. Like many people, he likes to read through information about world records for everything and I thought it would be interesting to know about the records held right here in the Show Me State.

I have collected lots of facts that I think you will enjoy knowing but my hope is that you yourself will collect some facts that you will be willing to share with me for a new edition of this book. If you find something I can use, I will list your name and hometown in the Contributors Page of the new book.

So, when you find something interesting, just go to my web site at:

www.RossMalone.com

Then find the "Contact" page. From there you can send me an email. I look forward to hearing from you!

Ross W. Malone

CONTENTS

The Book of Real

Missouri

Records

Show me the First, Last, Biggest, Smallest, Greatest, Worst, Strangest, Weirdest, and Funniest Things about our state!

Missouri's Biggest . . .

There are lots of truly big things in the Show Me State. In order to compare them in this book, they have been divided into several categories. The first is Big Buildings and Structures.

BIG BUILDINGS AND STRUCTURES:

LARGEST HOUSE:

On January 12, 2011 The *Christian County Headliner* carried a story about the construction of the largest home in America which was going up in Highlandville. 72,000+ square feet! This home, built of insulated concrete, will require little energy, and will be very resistant to tornadoes, earthquakes, fire, and insect damage. By comparison, the White House with three wings on six levels is only 55,000 square feet. This one has 15 bedrooms, and 14 baths. Its great hall is 1,970 square feet.

LARGEST ROCKING CHAIR:

On April 1, 2008 the world's largest rocking chair (four stories tall) was erected on old Route 66 at Fanning, MO.

BIGGEST HOT DOG CART:

In Union, Missouri the gourmet hot dog man, Marcus Daily, unveiled a gigantic replica of his regular cart on October 28, 2013. It's over 9 feet tall (not counting the giant umbrella), more than 23 feet long and over 12 feet wide!

BIGGEST THEATER:

The biggest theater in Missouri and the second largest in the world opened on New Year's Eve, 1929 in St. Louis. The Fox Theater seats 7500 people.

LARGEST PAINTING:

The "Mammoth Panorama of the Mississippi River" went on display in St. Louis way back on September 1, 1849. The oil painting was three-fourths of a mile long.

Some people might argue that the Wall of Fame depicting famous Missourians in Cape Girardeau is larger but it is actually a flood wall that has been decorated with multiple paintings rather than a single painting.

TALLEST NATIONAL MONUMENT:

The tallest national monument, St. Louis' Gateway Arch was completed on October 28, 1965. It is a special place with many special records of its own which will appear throughout this book. Some of the activities were daring but did not set any sort of records. For instance seven airplanes have flown through the Arch including the last one in 1977 which was at night with no lights on the Arch.

THE LARGEST INDOOR PARK:

On November 24, 1927 the elegant Pla-Mor Ballroom, the largest indoor amusement center in the country featuring a ballroom, bowling alley, billiard room, and an ice skating rink, opened to a crowd of 4,100. It was on Main Street in Kansas City.

THE LARGEST BREWERY:

On December 15, 1964 Anheuser-Busch in St. Louis became the first brewery in history to produce ten million barrels of beer in one year. Since that day it has remained the largest brewery in the world.

THE LARGEST STEAMBOAT:

The largest and most lavish steamer ever to navigate an inland waterway was launched on April 16, 1876. The steamer, *Grand Republic*, was built at Carondolet in December of 1875. It later burned while undergoing repairs there.

BIGGEST DRIVE-IN THEATER:

On January 2, 1955 construction began on a 16-acre drive-in theater on Page Avenue in St. Louis County. This popular place could show four movies at a time and had a concession stand in the middle which was a gathering place for teens and young families.

The Salon on the Grand Republic

OUR BIGGEST PEOPLE:

BIGGEST WOMAN:

March 9, 1872 was the birthday of The Missouri Giantess, Ella Ewing. Ella was considered the world's tallest female of her era. She would use her great height to earn a living as a sideshow attraction. Born a normal size in La Grange, she grew to a height which is in dispute. Her mother said that the last measurement she took was 8 ft., 4 in.

Ms. Ella Ewing with her parents

BIGGEST MAN:

Back on December 1, 1956, Hannibal native, Robert Earl Hughes, was on his way to New York this day for a TV appearance. He had to travel via air freight because they couldn't get him aboard a regular airliner. On that day, he weighed 1,041 pounds.

BIGGEST BABY:

The newspaper in Howell County reported on August 1, 1912 that Riley Fox, a baby in that place, was reported to be as large as a boy of ten, weighing 77 pounds. His parents said that whiskey was part of his daily food since he was two weeks old. Remember, reporting something doesn't make it true.

BIGGEST (FAKE) PEOPLE:

C.W. Beehler from Montesano (Jefferson Co.) announced on November 19, 1900 that he had discovered the fossil remains of three enormous humans. Found forty feet under the ground, they had skulls much larger than ours. It was thought that the giants must have been nine or ten feet tall. (Sasquatch or MoMo?)

BIGGEST ANIMALS:
The following are the largest fur-bearing animals known in Missouri.

Badger – Joe Closser got a 27 pound badger in Scotland County. (11-28-2011)

Beaver – Austin & Chase Minnick bagged a 72.2 pound beaver in Livingston County. (1-5-2012)

Bobcat – In Cooper County, Jason Maupin got a female weighing 31.8 pounds. (11-23-2011) Travis Ellis and Jonathon Wolf then got a 31.8 pound male in DeKalb county to tie the record. (11-30-2012)

BIGGEST ANIMALS: (Continued)

The following are the largest fur-bearing animals known in Missouri.

Coyote – Jim Palmer got a coyote in Mercer County that weighed 40.6 Pounds. (1-20-2012)

Gray Fox – The largest gray fox was bagged by Kenneth Naeger in St. Genevieve County. It weighed 9.8 pounds. (1-14-2011)

Mink – Jeff Thompson got a 5.2 pound mink in Ralls County. (1-16-2013)

Muskrat – Chuck Regnireb was in Boone County when he got his 3.6 pound muskrat. (1-29-2013)

Nutria – Bart Hiller got a big 10.4 pounder in Dunklin County. (1-18-2011)

Opossum – In Lafayette County, Kevin Whitworth got a 13.4 pound critter. (1-25-2012)

Otter – The biggest otter was taken by Jeff Bailey in Macon County. It weighed 30.8 pounds. (11-30-2012)

Raccoon – Chance Bailey got a 27.2 pounder in Macon County.

Red Fox – Steven Wiseman got an 11.9 pound fox in Cass County. (1-29-2013)

Did you notice how many of these records were set in very recent years?

Thanks to our farmers
and our Department of Natural Resources.

White Squirrels

BIGGEST WHITE SQUIRREL POPULATION:

If you are ever near Marionville, you will see the world's largest population of white squirrels. They aren't albinos but just a special natural variety. A few other communities around the nation have white squirrels but they aren't as big and there aren't as many. Marionville truly has something special.

BIGGEST RACK (DEER ANTLERS):

On November 10, 2001 Kevin Thomas of Sweet Springs shot a 33–point buck in Saline County.

OUR BIGGEST PARTY:

The Louisiana Purchase Exposition was an amazing event! It was so big that the International Olympic Games were just a small part of the proceedings. There were records set in many areas and they are located in every section of this book.

BIGGEST FERRIS WHEEL:

On May 24, 1904, the great Ferris Wheel at the World's Fair was tested. It stood 25 stories tall and could carry 2000 people. It had 36 cars and each of them was a large as a modern city bus. The axle was the largest piece of forged steel in the world.

1904 World's Fair Ferris Wheel

President Teddy Roosevelt visited the World's Fair and hob-knobbed with other world leaders. He met with Geronimo and was entertained by Will Rogers.

Many people saw electric lights for the first time and Semple Scott of St. Louis was granted permission to rent small electric cars similar to two-seat golf carts for getting around the World's Fair. They were called Electric Autochairs.

On July 6, 1904, the Democrat National Convention opened in St. Louis and tried to compete for attention with the World's Fair. To their chagrin, the people and the press paid more attention to the headlines coming from the Fair.

Even when the Fair was over it was still drawing crowds and making news. On May 11, 1906, a huge crowd was on hand to see the World's Fair Ferris wheel blown up.

To this day no one knows what happened to it. Some say it is buried in the park. Its scraps would be worth a fortune to anyone who could solve the mystery of its location.

Now, more than a hundred years after the big party, people are still interested in all of the amazing details. Be sure and watch for them as you read on in this book.

THE BIGGEST FARM:

This one becomes difficult to figure because farms are growing ever-larger and some Missouri farms are for crops, some for livestock and some for both. But there is one historic farm that must be considered.

By the time David Rankin of Tarkio died on October 18, 1910 he had created an amazing farm. Using the most modern methods, he had over 30,000 acres in cultivation. It was said to be the biggest farm operation in America. In addition to growing over a million bushels of corn per year, he had over 12,000 head of cattle and 25,000 hogs.

David Rankin's Mule barn (left) and Home
Photo, Courtesy Missouri State University

OTHER BIG

AGRICULTURE ACHIEVEMENTS:

HATCHERIES:

Missouri, at this writing, has thirteen commercial chick hatcheries. The average hatchery produces about 30 million birds per year. For a time, Clinton Missouri's Booth Hatchery was the largest in the world. It began in 1913 with the project of a high school boy, Royal Booth, who wanted to earn a little spending money and soon had three incubators including one that could hatch a million eggs at a time!

Three railroads had special cars designed to haul chicks from Booth Hatchery which, at its height, was producing 110 million chicks per year. Then as now Missouri's hatcheries produce baby chickens, ducks, quail, pheasant, turkeys and more.

RABBITS:

On December 19, 1917 the *Chillicothe Constitution* reported that C. C. Hoyt of Blue Mound, MO within the past week, had bought and sold 12,000 rabbits for an average of 16 and 2/3 cents each.

CABBAGE:

On December 22, 2011 Fourth Grader, Amber Trachsel of California, Missouri was being honored and presented with a scholarship for growing a 36 pound cabbage.

HOOPS:

In modern times this one is hard to understand but wooden hoops used to be big business. Back on February 8, 1888, Martin Zimpher of Antonia was seeking 50,000,000 hoop poles for which he offered the highest price. He needed them by spring in order to fill a contract.

Hoop poles had agricultural uses but mostly the ends of the poles were joined to form the hoops that ladies wore in their hoop skirts. Notice, Mr. Zimpher needed fifty million of them. However, by March 10, 1892 the hoop skirt fashion must have been winding down. On this day F.C. Vollmar of Antonia was hoping to buy one million hoop poles from local residents. A big drop from fifty million!

MUSHROOMS:

On October 24, 2005 Ty Whitmore of Kansas City found a "chicken of the woods" mushroom at Maysville. It broke as he tried to take it to his truck but the largest part was still big enough to set a world record at over 56 pounds!

The folks in Nevada, MO would claim that Ty Whitmore's mushroom is just a sprout compared to theirs. They have a giant **morel mushroom** 30 feet tall. Of course theirs is man-made and it's a morel. So I suppose Mr. Whitmore's record is safe for a while.

BIGGEST SOYBEAN YIELD:

The Show-Me State's Kip Cullers "obliterated" former world records with his soybean yield. He became the new world champ by harvesting over 139 bushels per acre in 2013.

FLIGHT:

This record may not exactly fit in this section of the book but it's certainly interesting and worth a mention. The biggest (longest) flight in the history of early aviation took place during the last seventeen days of July in 1929. Powered by a six-cylinder Challenger engine, the *St. Louis Robin*, piloted by Forest O'Brine and Dale Jackson, broke a world endurance record by flying in continuous circles over St. Louis. The craft's team was re-supplied 77 times with gasoline and necessities by a second plane flown by R. V. Chaffee and C. Ray Wassall.

MORE BIG THINGS IN MISSOURI:

BIGGEST BEARD:

On November 6, 1860 – Abraham Lincoln was elected President. He won only two counties in Missouri. Some counties gave him no votes at all. Nationwide, he failed to get a majority of the popular vote but he did get enough electoral votes. Poor Valentine Taplry felt certain that Lincoln would lose the election and he promised his Pike County friends that if Lincoln were to be elected, he would never shave again. His beard grew to over 12 ½ feet. The picture below shows his beard at just over half its eventual length.

Valentine Taplry

BIGGEST METEOR SHOWER:

Not just in Missouri but everywhere in this part of the solar system, November 13, 1833 was the night of the "Great Star Shower of 1833." It was said to be so bright that a newspaper could be read on the street. One writer says, "For nearly four hours the sky was literally ablaze." Many thought the end of the world had come.

BIGGEST PECAN:

Back in 1947, George James discovered an especially tasty type of pecan growing right there on his property near Brunswick. Its popularity grew and the James' prospered. So, in 1982, they created a huge concrete pecan and set it out for the world to see. The creation can be seen in front of the Nut Hut roadside stand on Highway 24, which is the location of the James' home. It weighs 12,000 pounds and is 7½ feet long or tall. Lots of other folks in the area now harvest pecans and yes, there is a Pecan Festival each October.

The Ponderous & Prodigious Pecan

BIGGEST GOOSE:

Her name Is Maxie. She stands 40 feet tall and has a wingspan of 61 feet and weighs over 4000 pounds. One day she flew in to Sumner's city park. To be more accurate, she was flying with the help of a lifting helicopter. Now wouldn't you think that a big fiberglass sculpture with outstretched 61 foot wings would have problems with the wind. Not Maxie! She swivels and turns to always face into the wind and that way is very aerodynamic.

Massive Maxie: The Hefty Honker

BIGGEST SCHOOL DISTRICT:

Surprise, it's not St. Louis or Kansas City. On December 14, 2011 the announcement was made that, with more than 50 schools and well over 24,000 students, the Springfield School District was now the largest in the state.

BIGGEST DOG BISCUIT:

Ten people in Joplin worked together to bake a 617 pound dog biscuit. And, yes, they set a world record that day. (July 8, 2011)

BIGGEST STEAMBOAT RACE:

The biggest and most famous steamboat race began on June 30, 1870 between the *Natchez* and the *Robert E. Lee* – a 1200 mile upstream race to St. Louis. The record of 3 days, 18 hours, and 14 minutes still stands today for steamboats.

BIGGEST BATTLE:

The largest battle west of the Mississippi was won by the Confederate forces at Wilson's Creek near Springfield on August 10, 1861. You can get a very interesting tour if you go past Battlefield Mall and watch for the signs.

BIGGEST DINNER:

On Christmas Day, 1934, 68,000 Depression Era poor were fed a free Christmas meal at the Kiel Auditorium in St. Louis.

BIGGEST DUST STORM:

November 11, 1933 – The "Black Blizzard," a giant dust storm blanketed Missouri and many other states. Of course this was because of "the dust bowl." Western real estate was still arriving in Missouri on the 12th as the gigantic storm continued.

BIGGEST EARTHQUAKE:

The largest earthquake ever to shake the contiguous states began on December 16, 1811. It was centered on the New Madrid Fault in Missouri. Often thought of as one quake, it was actually a series of many large quakes and hundreds of small ones over a period of many days. Lakes were instantly drained as other new ones were created. The Mighty Mississippi actually flowed backwards for a time. Steeples swayed and church bells rang as far away as the east coast.

BIGGEST PRIZE WINNERS:

The nation watched their television sets on April 6, 1957 as Teddy Nadler won another $32,000 dollars. That was an enormous amount in that day. Nadler was a contestant on the "$64,000 Question" TV show. He won a total of $152,000 all together because of his extensive knowledge of facts. However, he just couldn't use the facts that he memorized. He tried for many years with no success to pass the exam to be a postal employee.

Ernest Pullen was another unique winner. On September 17, 2010 he won a lottery prize worth more than a million dollars – for the second time!

BIGGEST CHIGGER:

On Highway 107 east of Stoutsville there is a giant chigger. It's a statue/sign at a place called Chigger Hill.

BIGGEST HAIR BALL:

At Henry Coffer's barber shop in Charleston you can find the world's largest ball of human hair. At the time of this writing, the ball weighs 167 pounds.

BIGGEST STRING BALL:

In Weston you can see the largest ball of string.

BIGGEST MILNOT CAN:

The biggest milnot can anywhere is in Senaca right at the state line.

BIGGEST GRASSHOPPERS:

Salibury's claim to fame is the pair of giant metal grasshoppers on highway 24.

BIGGEST PACIFIER:

Jefferson City has a gigantic baby pacifier made out of cigarette butts.

BIGGEST ICE CREAM CONE:

The state's largest soft serve in a cone is on 36th street in St. Joseph. You can't miss it because it's bright pink.

BIGGEST BILLIARD BALL:

In Tipton you will see a giant eight ball above the city. The ball also happens to be their water tower.

BIGGEST BANJO:

The biggest banjo you've ever seen is in Branson at the Grand Country Square. Just the neck on the thing is 47 feet long so it sticks out through a window of the building and reaches toward the street.

BIGGEST FORK:

Behind the Idea Center on Chesterfield in Springfield is a gleaming 35-foot stainless steel fork.

BIGGEST PAPER CUP

On North Glenstone Ave. in Springfield is the world's largest paper cup on the front of a paper cup factory.

BIGGEST HANDS:

There is a huge set of hands in prayer in Webb City.

BIGGEST FROG:

W. H. Croaker is a wonderful big bull frog that sits right next to old Route 66 in Waynesville. He's really an outcropping of limestone that was originally painted by a local art teacher and has been maintained by Waynesville H.S. students since then.

W. H. Croaker.

BIGGEST PRICE PAID FOR A PIE:

Rich Hill, Missouri is "Famous for the Fourth" and in 2013 it became even more famous. At the July 4 celebration they had the annual pie auction. Jerry Mumma paid $3,100 for a banana-peanut butter pie on a pretzel crust. The pie was made by his granddaughter, Jara Mumma.

BIGGEST CONVOY:

Law enforcement officials in Joplin reported escorting 234 semi-trucks through Downtown Joplin on September 28, 2013. The event set a World Record as the caravan stretched out for more than 15 miles!

KANSAS CITY GIANTS:

If you're in the Kansas City area you can see the following BIGGEST attractions:

The **BIGGEST SHUTTLECOCKS** can be found at the Nelson-Atkins Art Museum.

The **BIGGEST SEWING NEEDLE** is sticking through a GIANT BUTTON at 404 Eighth St. in Downtown K.C.

At 1219 Union, look up. You'll see the world's **BIGGEST CAP GUN.**

Finally, at the Western Missouri Soccer League fields you may be amazed to see the world's **LARGEST SOCCER BALL.**

You can see the **BIGGEST BOOKS** imaginable. They're about a city block long and are part of the Library building on West 10th Street. Each book is 25 feet high!

Watch out for the **BIGGEST SPIDER.** He's at the Kemper Museum of Contemporary Art.

BIGGEST FISH:
The following are some of Missouri's biggest fish catches in each species:

Largemouth Bass – Mark Bushong of Gainsville caught a 13 lb. 14 oz. beauty at Bull Shoals Lake.
Smallmouth Bass – Kevin S. Clingan of Springfield caught on weighing 7 ob. 2 oz. while fishing at Stockton Lake.
Spotted Bass – Gene Arnaud from Branson used a pole and line to catch a 7 ½ pounder at Table Rock.
Striped Bass – The record here goes to James Cuningham of Fordland. He caught a 60 lb 9 oz. monster with a pole and line at Bull Shoals Lake.
White Bass – Scott Flood from Billings was fishing at Table Rock Lake when he caught his 5 lb. 6 oz. white bass.
Yellow Bass – Jessica Murray from St. Peters was fishing the Sandy Slough when she caught a 9 oz. yellow bass. Yes, that is a record.
Bluegill – Robert Michael Giovaini of Columbia MO caught a 3 pounder in a farm pond.
Bowfin – Clois Coomer of Chaffee, MO caught a 19 pounder with a pole and line in Duck Creek.
Bigmouth Buffalo – Dr. W. J. Long of Poplar Bluff used a pole and line to catch his 56 lb. buffalo in Loch-Loma Lake. Dennis Shafer of Stover was snagging when he pulled in a 53 pounder for the Lake of the Ozarks.
Black Buffalo – Barry Caldwell from Puxico was using a bow and arrow when he got his 59 lb. 4 oz. buffalo from Duck Creek. Marty Ray Yount from Hiram pulled a 53 pounder from Wappapello Lake.
Smallmouth Buffalo - Lucas Dement of Ste. Genevieve was fishing with a bow and arrow at Duck Creek when he caught his smallmouth that weighed 46 ½ pounds. Allen Schweiss from IL was using a pole and line when he pulled a 36 lb. 12 oz. smallmouth for the Lake of the Ozarks.

BIGGEST FISH (Continued):

Black Bullhead – Ron Miller from Jefferson City was at Binder Lake when he caught his 4 lb. 11 oz. bullhead with a pole and line.

Brown Bullhead – Greg L Clanahan from Poplar Bluff holds the record here with a 3 lb. 3 oz. brown that he took from Lock-Loma Lake.

Yellow Bullhead – John Irvin from Drexel was fishing the Old Drexel Lake when he caught his 6 lb. 6 oz. yellow.

Bighead Carp – Gene Swope from Excelsior Springs was snagging at the Lake of the Ozarks when he pulled in his 106 lb. carp. Kyle Schneider from Ballwin was also at the Lake of the Ozarks but he used a pole and line to catch his 80 pounder.

Common Carp – A 55 lb. carp was brought in by Tim Dernosek from Blue Springs. He used his bow and arrow at Lake Lotawana. Russell Tarr from Moberly caught his 50 pounder with a pole and line at Rothwell Park Lake.

Grass Carp – Donald Atterberry from Memphis, MO holds the record for a grass carp. His arrow brought back a 71 lb. 4 oz. fish from Lake Showme. Jim Shull of Trenton used a pole and line to hook his 69 pounder at the Crowder State Park.

Highfin Carpsucker – Derek DePew of DeSoto was fishing with a bow in the Meramec River when he shot his 1 lb. 6 oz. record carpsucker.

River Carpsucker – Cody Chaney from Belton used an arrow to bring in his 5 ½ pounder from the Lake of the Ozarks. Nicholas Wray from Harrisonville was fishing the South Grand River with a pole and line when he got his 2 lb. 3 oz. fish.

Blue Catfish – A 130 lb. blue was pulled from the Missouri River by Greg Bernal of Florissant. He used a pole and line. Azel Goans from Lowery City got a 117 pounder from the Osage River on a trotline. This one was a world record.

White Catfish – The record here is held by Robert Maddux from Holden whose 7 lb. 4 oz. fish was caught with a bankline.

BIGGEST FISH (Continued):

Channel Catfish – Gerald Siebenmorgen from Independence holds the record for channel cats. He was using a pole and line at Lake Jacomo when he caught his 34 lb. 10 oz. trophy. Monte Hoover had a bankline that hooked a 29 lb. 14 oz. fish.

Flathead Catfish – Robert Neal Davidson of Mokane was fishing the Missouri River with a bank pole when he caught his 99 lb. flathead. Scott Brown of Odessa caught a 77 ½ pounder in Montrose Lake.

White Catfish – The record here is held by Robert Maddux from Holden whose 7 lb. 4 oz. fish was caught with a bankline.

Black Crappie – John Horstman from Mokane used a pole and line to catch his 5 lb. crappie in a private farm pond. Skipper Autley from Drexel used a yo-yo at Lisle Lake and got a 3 lb 3oz. black.

White Crappie – Samuel Barbee from Poplar Bluff caught a 4 lb. 9 oz white in a farm pond with a pole and line.

Freshwater Drum – Ronald Wagner from Iowa was fishing at the Lake of the Ozarks with a pole and line when he caught his 40 lb. 8 oz. drum. Kenneth Hoener from Hermann was gigging at the same lake when he caught his 28 ½ pounder.

American Eel – Steven Buerk from Sullivan holds this record. He was fishing with a pole and line in the Meramec River when he got his 4 ½ pounder. David Ward from Advance missed the record by only 6 oz. but his fish still holds the record for limb line.

Alligator Gar – Larry Wolfe from Chaffee must have been surprised when his arrow brought in a 127 lb. monster from a diversion channel off the Mississippi.

In March and April of 1942 newspapers across the nation were reporting that J.B. Shelton of Sulphur Springs had caught a 200 pound gar. They did not tell what kind of gar or what method he used to catch the giant.

Spotted Gar – Eric Whitehead from Puxico was at Wappapello Lake with his bow when he got his record 9 lb. 15 oz. fish. Brent Meyer from New Haven used a pole and line in nearby Boeuf Creek to get his 6 lb. gar.

BIGGEST FISH (Continued):

Goggle-eye – This fish is also known as the Ozark Bass, the Rock Bass, and the Shadow Bass. William Rod from Kirkwood caught a 2 lb. 12 oz. goggle-eye in the Big Piney River with a pole and line.

Goldeye – Jonnie Lay was using a thowline in the Mississippi and caught a 1 lb. 15 oz. fish. Rachel Davis from Climax Springs caught her 1 lb. 12 oz. goldeye in the Lake of the Ozarks with a pole and line.

Skipjack Herring – Roger Gerloff from Jefferson City was fishing the Osage Rover with a pole and line when he got his 1 lb. 11 oz. skipjack.

Muskellunge – The Lake of the Ozarks produced a 41 lb. 2 oz. fish for Gene Snelling of Camdenton. He used a pole and line.

Tiger Muskellunge – The record holder here is a 22 pounder caught with a pole and line by Ned Posinki of Springfield.

Paddlefish – Missouri's Official State Aquatic Animal is actually a freshwater member of the shark family. George Russell of DeSoto snagged one at Table Rock Lake that weighed 139 lbs. 4 oz. James Godfrey from Kansas City used a pole and line to catch one at Lake Jacomo that weighed in at 108 ½ pounds.

Yellow Perch – Vince Elfrink of Walnut Shade used a pole and line at Bull Shoals to catch his 1 lb. 11 oz prize.

Chain Pickerel – Duck Creek produced a 6 lb. 3 oz. record for Gordon Thornton from Campbell. He used a bankline. With a pole and line George Burlbaw from Farmington got a 5 lb. 1 oz. pickerel from the spillway at Clearwater Lake.

Grass Pickerel – will Dougherty from Mill Spring used a pole and line in a farm pond to catch his record 1 lb. 3 oz. pickerel.

Northern Pike – The 18 lb. 3 oz. record fish was caught in Stockton Lake with a pole and line by Gene Moore of Golden City.

Quillback – Donald Morey (from Lafayette) used a pole and line in the North Fabius River to catch his 2 lb. 12 oz. prize. Kurt Kysar from O'Fallon gigged a 1 lb. 14 oz. fish in the Big River.

BIGGEST FISH (Continued):

Black Redhorse – Andy Foster from Poplar Bluff must have been amazed when he gigged a 9 lb. 13 oz. redhorse in the Current River. The pole and line record is a 1 lb. 8 oz. fish taken by Mike Jackson from Bourbon. He was fishing near home on the Meramec River.

Golden Redhorse – Henry Glass from Tunas, MO used a pole and line to catch a 5 lb. 1 oz. redhorse in the Niangua River. But Ron Jones from Nixa just took his hands and grabbed (noodled) a 10 lb. 15 oz. fish from Bull Creek.

River Redhorse – Frank Harding from Nixa was also noodling (grabbing) fish in the Elk River when he pulled out a 17 lb. 1 oz. prize! The pole and line record is held by Buck Hennessy from Jefferson City. He got a 9 lb. 10 oz. river redhorse from the Osage River.

Shorthead Redhorse – Gerald Wright of Independence got the shorthead record when he used a pole and line to bring in a 2 lb. 14 oz. fish from Truman Lake.

Silver Redhorse – Teresa Meadors from Halfway took a pole and line record maker from the Sac River. It weighed 5 lb. 10 oz. Jordan Brown of Cuba, MO was gigging in the Bourbeuse River when he speared a 9 lb. 13 oz. prize.

Sauger – Buck Hennessy was mentioned above. He also holds the record for sauger by pulling a 5 lb. 1 oz. beauty from the Osage River.

Gizzard Shad – Brian Taylor from Poplar Bluff used a pole and line in the Black River to catch a 1 lb. 6 oz. shad. This fresh water member of the salmon family outweighed the previous record by six ounces. Michael Schoening of Owensville was gigging in the Bourbeuse River when he got his prize fish of 2 lb. 5 oz.

Lake Sturgeon – Alex Whitelaw, Joseph Drohr Sr. & Jr. together pulled in a 53 lb. sturgeon. They had a throw line in the Missouri River. This was well over 60 years ago and the lake sturgeon is now an endangered species.

BIGGEST FISH (Continued):

Shovelnose Sturgeon – James Dockery of Queen City used a pole and line in the Des Moines River to catch a 5 pounder. Joe McMullen of Sullivan used a trotline in the Osage River to catch a 2 lb. 3 oz. fish.

Blue Sucker – Randy L. Christian of Savannah, MO got a 9 lb. 14 oz. fish with a pole and line in the Missouri River. Dan Gamble from Nixa grabbed a 7 lb. 6 oz. sucker in the Bull Creek. Do you think it went to the Nixa Sucker Days Festival?

Northern Hog Sucker – David Cletcher from Ellsinore was using a pole and line in the Current River when he caught a 3 lb. 5 oz. prize. Also in the Current River, Stephen Rowland of Poplar Bluff gigged a 2 lb. 4 oz. fish.

Spotted Sucker – Douglas Stilts of Wappapello snagged a 2 lb. 1 oz. record fish at Wappapello Lake.

White Sucker – James Baker of Reeds Springs was using a pole and line at Lake when he caught his 4 ½ pound record.

Green Sunfish – Paul Dilley of Springfield used a pole and line to catch a 2 lb. 2 oz. green at Stockton Lake.

Redear Sunfish – Glenda Gollaher from Overland caught her 2 lb. 7 oz. sunfish at the Whetstone Creek.

Brook Trout – Brodrick Glessner from Sunrise Beach caught a 1 lb. 14 oz. brook trout near his home at the Lake of the Ozarks.

Brown Trout – Scott Sandusky from Arnold caught a 28 lb. 12 oz. brown trout at Lake Taneycomo! He used a pole and line.

Rainbow Trout – An 18 lb. 1 oz. rainbow was caught by Jason Harper of Neosho. He used a pole and line at Roaring River. Robert Brownfield from St. Louis used a throwline to catch his 15 lb. 6 oz. rainbow at Lake Taneycomo.

Walleye – With a line and pole, Gerry Partlow from Linneus caught a 21 ob. 1 oz. walleye at Bull Shoals. At the South Fabius River, Travis Moore from Palmyra caught a 5 lb. 13 oz. fish on a trotline.

Warmouth – Using a pole and line Tony Fincher from Holcomb caught a 1 lb. 4 oz. in a farm pond.

ST. LOUIS GIANTS:

We saw Kansas City's giant things. Now, if you're in the on the other side of the state and in the St. Louis area you can see the following BIGGEST attractions:

The **BIGGEST TURTLES** in the state are on the lawn in Turtle Park across from the St. Louis Zoo.

In the Cherokee Street antique district you will see the **BIGGEST INDIAN** statue ever. The big guy is so ugly, however, that even the sculptor who made it doesn't like it.

The Sappington Farmers Market has a **GIANT FARMER** with his giant son.

Downtown on Eighth Street there is a **GIANT'S HEAD**. It's so big you can walk around inside and peek out of its eyes.

The **BIGGEST TEETH** anywhere are at the Dental Health Theater on Laclede's Landing.

At the headquarters building for the International Shoe Company in Clayton you can see the **BIGGEST SHOE**. It's a big high-heel slipper which happens to be constructed of regular sized high-heel shoes.

The **BIGGEST EYEBALL** in the world is at the Laumeier Sculpture Park in Sunset Hills. It's creepy but really cool!

The **BIGGEST CATERPILLAR** and the **BIGGEST BUTTERFLY** can be found out in Chesterfield at the Faust Park. They are at the entrance to the Missouri Botanical Garden's Butterfly House.

Also in Chesterfield there is a sculpture of a gigantic man awakening from his sleep and rising up out of he ground. He's 70 feet long and 17 feet tall!

Missouri's Smallest

SMALLEST PEOPLE:

Way down in Hornersville, in the late 1800s, there was a very small and very special couple of people. They were known to be the world's smallest married couple. The most famous of the pair was W. H. "Major" Ray. At 44 inches tall, he was a popular circus attraction. His wife, Jennie, wasn't as outgoing as Major but she was special also because she was only 37 inches tall.

At one time, the Brown Shoe Company in St. Louis was having trouble keeping the boys they hired to portray Buster Brown because they kept growing up. Major approached the company and suggested they hire a small man who was already a professional entertainer and he was then hired to be Buster Brown for many years. He always sang that he and his dog, Tige, lived in a shoe.

When Major and Jennie retired from the circus they opened a general store in Hornersville and operated it with their partner who happened to be the giant from the same circus. They must have been quite a sight in their little store! If you would like to read more about Major and Jenny, get Laura Ford's book, *For the Love of Jennie*.

SMALLEST JAIL SENTENCE:

On August 8, 1833, Pulaski County Court charged Archibald McDonald with maiming William Black in a gun fight. He was sentenced to "one minute" in the county jail.

SMALLEST (SHORTEST) TERM AS PRESIDENT:

On August 11, 1807, David Rice Atchison of Liberty and Platt City, MO was born and was destined to become the President of the United States. Atchison was a "border ruffian," lawyer, soldier, and U.S. Senator. He is largely responsible for the Transcontinental Railway going through Missouri and Kansas. We remember him however as being the acting President of our nation for only one day. When the President-Elect wanted to postpone his inauguration, someone had to serve for that one day and the Vice-President was not yet inaugurated either so Atchison, as leader of the Senate became President until the new POTUS was sworn in.

SMALLEST PROFESSIONAL BASEBALL PLAYER:

On August 19, 1951, Eddie Gaedel played for the St. Louis Browns. Since he was only three feet, seven inches tall, that made him the smallest person to every play professional baseball. He batted only once but, because of his small strike zone, he was walked and received a standing ovation from the crowd.

The Browns didn't have a uniform small enough to fit Gaedel so they borrowed one from the team's bat boy and put the number "1/8" on the back. It's interesting to note that the bat boy whose uniform Gaedel used was named Bill Dewitt and he is the present-day owner of the St. Louis Cardinals.

On August 22, 1951, Eddie Gaedel was back in the headlines again. Just days after Brown's owner Bill Veeck sent the 3' 7" midget up to bat for the Browns, Gaedel was arrested in Cincinnati. Police there had mistaken him for a juvenile and busted him for curfew violation.

SMALLEST COUNTY

On February 8, 1861, Worth County was established. It was the last to be formed, the smallest in size, and the smallest in population.

SMALLEST RAILROAD:

Glencoe, Missouri has something as great as it is tiny. The Wabash, Frisco, and Pacific Railroad operates a little 12-inch gauge railroad that runs with actual steam engines. The WF&P RR was organized in 1939 and these railroad enthusiasts build the little trains and the tracks, roundhouses, water towers, and everything else needed to take you on a trip through the Ozarks countryside. They do charge $4.00 but it's worth it. Kids, parents, and grandparents of all ages show up for this and enjoy it. You can hop aboard the WF&P RR on Sunday afternoons from May through October. Please remember, this is not a commercial operation. It's just a bunch of nice people wanting to have fun.

SMALLEST CHURCHES:

At Mt. Vernon there is a very tiny church. Shepherd's Field Wedding Chapel is said to be the Smallest Chapel in use in the state of Missouri. Some will tell you that it's the smallest in the United States. The Chapel is 6'x10' outside dimensions and can hold a wedding party of 10. It may have really been intended to be used as a backdrop for outside weddings. It's on Farm Road 2137 so you will need a good map or you can google the directions.

There is a smaller and better church between Hannibal and Bowling Green near Frankford. This little white frame building has windows and everything. Follow Route C out of Frankford for about five miles.

SMALLEST BANK:

At Long Lane there sits a building which was for years, a genuine working bank. The First State Bank of Long Lane was incorporated in 1910 and was an important part of the little community. It even survived the Great Depression and a robbery in the 1930s. It couldn't survive the automobile however and locals began to drive to bigger institutions in Buffalo. At about 12 feet by 20 feet, it really is tiny and, if you happen to be driving down Highway 32, watch for it.

Missouri's Firsts

Missouri and our history are full of first! Once again we have put them into categories with Aviation Firsts first! As you read please remember, all of these were Missouri records but almost every one of them was also a world record.

AVIATION:

FIRST PROPELLING DEVICE FOR AIRCRAFT:

On May 31, 1830, Dr. Claude George Brun filed a patent for a muscle-powered propelling device for balloons and boats in St. Louis County.

FIRST BALLOON RIDE:

May 17, 1836 – Richard Clayton ascended from a lot at Fourth and Market streets at 6:30 p.m., making St. Louis's first balloon ascension. He charged admission to watch but most folks just watched from a couple of blocks away.

FIRST GIRL IN A BALLOON:

On October 9, 1841 Miss Day, a fourteen-year-old St. Louis girl, became St. Louis's first girl to ascend in a balloon. Mr. S. Hobart took her on a ten-mile trip.

FIRST BALLOON DISTANCE RECORD:

The second balloon ever to fly in St. Louis flew all the way to New York! On July 1-2, 1859 John Wise established a world distance record, traveling 809 miles in the *Atlantic*, a 65,000-cubic-foot helium balloon. Read more about this flight in Bob Priddy's book, *Across Our Wide Missouri*.

FIRST BALLOON DEATH:

Flying in those old-fashioned balloons could be dangerous. On October 13, 1877, Lizzie Wise drew a crowd as she ascended in her balloon from the Grand Avenue Baseball Park in St. Louis. A stiff wind grabbed the balloon and she was whisked away. She was found the next day in Illinois, hanging from a treetop, unharmed. Several years later, on August 29, 1896 a large crowd at the St. Louis County Fair watched as the famed aeronaut, Mademoiselle Victoria LeRoy fell to her death from a gaily decorated balloon.

FIRST POLICE AIRCRAFT:

The very first "bear in the air" was on May 24, 1904. The St. Louis County Constable became the very first to try and spot speeders from the air. He ascended in a balloon but couldn't spot any "scorchers."

FIRST FLYBOYS CONVENTION:

On October 4-5, 1904, the International Aeronautical Congress was held in the Transportation Hall during the Louisiana Purchase Exhibition of 1904 for leading scientists to discuss aeronautical accomplishments and possibilities.

FIRST CONTROLLED FLIGHT:

In was an exciting day at the World's Far when, on October 25, 1904, Captain Thomas Scott Baldwin's airship demonstration at the Louisiana Purchase Exhibition of 1904 was St. Louis's first exposure to controlled flight. A. Roy Knabenshue operated the powered balloon, maneuvering it in the shape of an "S." He flew for 37 minutes and climbed to 2,000 feet above the fairgrounds.

Baldwin's Airship Flown by Roy Knabenshue

FIRST GROUND-TO-AIR COMMUNICATION:

Paul Knabenshue, A. W. McQueen, and Will S. Forman ascended in a balloon at 3:15 p.m. on November 11, 1904 and received the first wireless telegraph between the ground and the air in the United States. During their trip, the three men received 20 telegraph messages.

FIRST FLYING CLUB:

The Aero Club of St. Louis was formed on January of 1907.

FIRST AMERICAN BALLOON RACE (Distance):

On October 21-26, 1907, the James Gordon Bennett Cup International Balloon Race was held in St. Louis the first time that the race was held in America. The race was won by Germany's *Pommern*, piloted by Oscar Erbsloeh and assisted by Helm Clayton. They traveled 867.4 miles to Asbury Park, New Jersey.

FIRST AMERICAN BALLOON RACE (Speed):

The first ever air race was held in St. Louis, Missouri, on May 27, 1908. The participants piloted the only 4 airships in the U.S. around a course located at Forest Park. Two of the pilots went off-course due to strong winds, and the other 2 successfully completed the course, and divided the $5,000 prize.

NO RECORD, *BUT WORTH MENTIONING*:

Albert Bond Lambert was the eighth balloon pilot in America and the person who, in 1920, bought, cleared, and leveled a flying field that is now an international airport at St. Louis. On November 19, 1908 He was in the balloon "Yankee" when it landed in Northeastern Georgia, 450 miles from its take off point in St. Louis. Albert Bond Lambert, the President of the St. Louis Aero Club, and pilot A.E. Honeywell came up short by 25 miles in their attempt to set a new distance record.

FIRST WOMEN TO FLY IN A BALLOON:

On July 16, 1909, Ada Miller, Mary Van Fertig, and Mrs. Honeywell ascended with Harry E. Honeywell to become the first women in St. Louis to lift off in a balloon.

FIRST HELICOPTER:

Since the days of Leonardo Da Vinci people dreamed of making helicopters. A real helicopter actually flew for the very first time on July 3, 1910. The Holbrook Helicopter Aeroplane group of Monett and Joplin built a strange aluminum combination of airplane and helicopter. It flew at an altitude of about 5 feet for about 6 minutes on this day. Remember, the Wright brothers flew the very first airplane just 6 ½ years earlier. This was almost a half-century before small helicopters began being used in the Korean War!

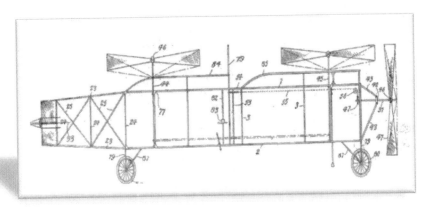

The Patent Office Drawing of the Holbrook Helicopter Aeroplane.

FIRST LONG FLIGHT IN AN AIRPLANE:

On September 10, 1910, Captain Thomas Scott Baldwin made St. Louis's first extensive flight in an airplane with his plane, the *Red Devil*. In his flight, Captain Baldwin flew under the Eads Bridge and the McKinley Bridge, much to the delight of spectators.

Baldwin's Red Devil Aeorplane

FIRST U. S. PRESIDENT TO FLY:

On October 8-18, 1910, St. Louis hosted the International Aeronautic Tournament, which included airplane tournaments, stunts, and races. It was here that Theodore Roosevelt became the first President to fly. He came to Aviation Field in St. Louis on October 11, 1910 for the experience. His pilot was Arch Hoxsey.

FIRST NATIONAL AIR SHOW:

From November 17th to the 24th, 1910 – The Aero Club of St. Louis hosted the first-ever National Aero Show.

FIRST BENNETT CUP RACE:

On October 17, 1910, The James Gordon Bennett Cup International Balloon Race was held in St. Louis. The United States won, with Pilot Alan R. Hawley and assistant Augustus Post flying in the *America II*.

FIRST PHONE CALL TO AN AIRCRAFT:

This happened on October 17, 1911 when Bernays Johnson held the first pilot/passenger conversation with Howard Gill over an aerophone.

FIRST MIDGET IN THE AIR:

It was October 18, 1911. A little person named Master Gabriel became the first midget to fly in a plane.

AVIATION PIONEERS IN SOUTHWEST MISSOURI:

Surprisingly, some of the best early powered flight took place in places like Monett, Neosho, and Joplin. Hugh Armstrong Robinson was the third man in history to fly an airplane. He was right after his two teachers, Orville and Wilber Wright. He is no doubt a factor in the interest in flight around his home in Neosho. On June 30, 1911 The *Monett Times* stated, "If you fail to attend our Fourth of July celebration next Tuesday you will ever regret it." Does that sound like a threat? It wasn't intended that way, They knew that crowds of people would want to come and see the new aeroplanes.

Earlier that year the paper said that Monett expected to be "flying high." They were pinning their hopes on the new airplane industry and the Monett Aeroplane Company. The paper stated, "...a smart start here will no doubt develop into an immense industry in a few years." Well the aircraft industry did thrive in Missouri but it turned out to be in St. Louis and Kansas City.

So what about that Fourth of July Celebration in Monett? It was a rousing big event with large crowds there to see the local druggist make his solo flight in the newest version of the DeChenne Bi-Plane. See the following picture of the event.

An Early DeChenne Bi-Plane in Monett

FIRST AIRMAIL FLIGHT:

It was October 4, 1911 when Walter Brookins piloted the first airmail flight in St. Louis. He took off from Kinloch Park and landed in Fairgrounds Park, where the mail was taken to the downtown post office for delivery.

FIRST PARACHUTE JUMP:

Imagine the excitement on March 1, 1912 as Captain Albert S. Berry became the first person in the world to jump from an airplane with a parachute. He landed at Jefferson Barracks. (St. Louis)

FIRST BEER DELIVERY BY PLANE:

Tony Jannus made a historic trip on December 15, 1912. He became the first person ever to deliver beer by airplane. He flew the bubbly cargo from St. Louis to the Mayor of New Orleans.

Tony Jannus on his Benoist Aeroplane

The Lemp brewery strapped a case of beer onto the fabric wing right behind the pilot. When he landed that evening after the first leg of his journey almost half of the beer bottles were empty. By the time he got to New Orleans all of the beer was gone but the mayor smiled and acted pleased in front of all the cameras. A good politician.

FIRST SCHEDULED AIRLINE SERVICE:

On January 1, 1914, Missourians Tom Benoist and Tony Jannus began the first scheduled passenger airline service in America. After testing their flying boat at Creve Coeur Lake in St. Louis County, they began flying a scheduled route between Tampa and St. Petersburg.

Replica of the Benoist Flying Boat, America's first airliner.

FIRST FLYING SCHOOL:

The War Department chose the Missouri Aeronautical Society Balloon School as the first school in the nation to be officially recognized by the War Department as a training school for the United States Army Aeronautical Corps which eventually became the U.S. Air Force. This was on June 5, 1917.

FIRST SKYWRITER:

The very first skywriter was seen over St. Louis spelling out "Lucky Strike" on May 19, 1923. Old-timers will know that is not an ad for bowling or baseball.

FIRST STEP TO AN AIR NATIONAL GUARD:

June 23, 1923 – On this date the Army formed the 100th Observation Squadron which has evolved into the Missouri Air National Guard.

FIRST PUBLIC NOTICE OF CHARLES LINDBERGH:

Charles Lindbergh would dominate aviation headlines for decades but it was on July 1, 1925 that he began to be noticed by the average citizen. The St. Louis Flying Club announced that as a part of their stunt flying show, they would have the only many ever to have survived a mid-air collision. He was relatively unknown but those who knew him called him 'Lucky Lindy'. As you read through this book, you will see many more accomplishments by this remarkable and sometimes controversial man.

FIRST AIRMAIL FLIGHT FOR LINDBERGH:

A test run for the new air mail service between St. Louis and Chicago was flown on April 14, 1926. Charles Lindbergh flew the first run. His employer, Robertson Aircraft Company of St. Louis, would grow into American Airlines. Lindbergh crashed twice on this St. Louis to Chicago run. September 30, 1926 – with engine failure in his mail plane, Lucky Lindy glided in for a safe landing in a farm field. Two weeks earlier his plane ran out of gas near Chicago and he was forced to bail out.

On October 15, 1926, the Robertson Aircraft Corporation began its schedule airmail service, with Charles Lindberg piloting the first plane from Maywood Field, Chicago, to Lambert Field, St. Louis. Three weeks later he survived a fourth parachute jump. His plane ran out of gas over Bloomington, Illinois.

FIRST AIRMAIL FLIGHT FOR LINDBERGH: (Continued)

In order to compete for a huge prize and to meet an unattained challenge, Lindbergh convinced some St. Louis aviation enthusiasts to build a specially modified plane for him. Then on May 10, 1927, Charles Lindbergh flew *The Spirit of St. Louis* from San Diego to St. Louis and set a speed record doing it. After a day's rest, he flew to New York and set another record. His next flight was from New York to Paris which was also something of a record.

Ten days later everyone across Missouri and the world listened to their radios for news of *The Spirit of St. Louis.*

FIRST SOLO TRANS-ATLANTIC FLIGHT:

On May 21, 1927, with Missouri backing, Charles Lindbergh's plane: The Spirit of St. Louis

Ten days later everyone across Missouri and the world listened to their radios for news of *The Spirit of St. Louis,* completed the solo journey across the Atlantic.

On June 17, 1927, Lindbergh flew *The Spirit of St. Louis* back to its home at Lambert Flying Field. Twenty planes accompanied Lindbergh and steamboat and railroad whistles shrieked their welcomes.

On August 17, 1927, having arrived in town in *The Spirit of St. Louis*, Charles Lindbergh dedicated the new Municipal Airport in Kansas City. A crowd of 25,000 was on hand. On news that Charles Lindbergh was returning home from his goodwill tour of Mexico and South America, 100,000 crowded the St. Louis riverfront to welcome him on February 14, 1928. On seeing the crowd, Lindbergh put on a stunt flying show for them.

Lindbergh received many honors and awards but the highest came on March 21, 1928 when President Coolidge presented Lucky Lindy with the Congressional Medal of Honor. *The Spirit of St. Louis* went to the Smithsonian Museum in Washington D.C.

FIRST FEMALE PILOT:

It was an exciting day on June 28, 1927, when Marian Greene became the first female pilot in the state as she flew a solo sortie from Lambert Field.

FIRST HIGH ALTITUDE DEATH:

Captain Hawthorne Gray beat the record altitude mark in his balloon, albeit at the cost of his life. The record was held by an airplane pilot at 38,704 feet, but, on November 4, 1927, Gray marked 40,000 feet in his log. Soon thereafter, a quick change in air pressure knocked him unconscious, and he suffocated.

FIRST FLYING COW:

Elm Farm Ollie was a famous cow after February 18, 1930. She became the first cow to fly in an airplane. She took off from Bismarck, Missouri and flew to St. Louis.

FIRST MAN TO MILK A COW IN THE AIR:

On the day that Elm Farm Ollie flew to St. Louis. Elsworth Bunce became the first man to milk a cow in the air. He milked Ollie and then the milk was put into paper containers and dropped by parachute as an advertising stunt.

FIRST FEMALE PILOT'S LICENSE:

On May 3, 1930, Laura Ingalls became the first licensed woman pilot in St. Louis. No, this was not the other famous Missourian, Laura Ingalls Wilder.

FIRST COAST-TO-COAST PASSENGER SERVICE:

Trans World Airlines established the first coast-to-coast all-air passenger service on October 25, 1930. The planes flew from New York to Kansas City for an overnight stop and then on to Los Angeles. Total trip time was 36 hours.

FIRST AIR CARGO:

On August 6, 1931, TWA became the first airline to carry cargo. On this date a shipment of livestock was flown from St. Louis to New Jersey.

FIRST RECORD FOR INVERTED FLIGHT:

On August 27, 1933, Lieutenant Tito Falconi flew his open-cockpit airplane from St. Louis to Joliet upside down. He was happy to set the record for inverted flight but was a little worried also because one of the straps that held him in broke along the way.

FIRST 1000 MPH FLIGHT OF A MISSOURI AIRCRAFT:

The McDonnell Douglas Voodoo established the speed record for airplanes at 1,207.6 mph on December 12, 1957.

FIRST AMERICAN SPACESHIP:

On May 5, 1961, Alan Shepard became the first American to go into space. His Mercury capsule is one of twenty spaceships to be built in St. Louis by McDonnell-Douglas.

FIRST SABATAGED AIRLINER:

Continental Airlines Flight 11 was headed for Kansas City when it blew up and fell near Unionville, MO on May 22, 1962. A passenger blew up the plane committing insurance fraud. This was the first time in history that an airliner was sabotaged.

FIRST STEALTH BOMBER BASE:

The first B-2 stealth bomber, *The Spirit of Missouri*, swooped in from the sky to land at its new home, Whiteman Air Force Base on December 17, 1993. This base at Knob Noster is home to the entire stealth bomber fleet and planes from here fly round-trip missions to all parts of the world.

FIRST SOLO AROUND-THE-WORLD BALLOON FLIGHT:

Steve Fossett, the Washington U. graduate who based his flying operations at that St. Louis institution, completed the first solo around-the-world flight on March 3, 2005. The millionaire balloonist and adventurer held 116 records in five different sports. He was killed on September 3, 2007 when his private plane crashed in the desert.

FIRST TOWNS & VILLAGES:

FIRST PIONEER SETTLEMENT IN MISSOURI:

Way back on June 10, 1702, a mission was founded on the Mississippi at the mouth of the River Des Peres. This was the first European settlement in what is now Missouri. This mission at the "River of the Fathers" lasted only about one year. The settlement was abandoned in 1704, 63 years before Auguste Chouteau founded St. Louis and about 20 years before the settling of Ste. Genevieve.

FIRST PIONEER DEATH AND BURIAL:

On August 1, 1702, Missionary Pierre Francois Pinet died at a village established by the Jesuits on the north bank of the River Des Peres in what is now St. Louis. Pinet's death and burial are the first recorded on Missouri soil. This settlement is the one noted directly above.

FIRST EUROPEAN SETTLEMENT:

Fort Orleans, first European post in the Missouri Valley, was built by the French explorer Etienne Véniard De Bourgmond on the Missouri River, in the western part of the state a few miles above the mouth of the Grand River, in 1723. He chose a spot directly across the river from a village of the Missouri Indians. This trading post lasted only a short time.

FIRST PERMANENT SETTLEMENT:

The people at Old Mines, Missouri point out that their community was established by French miners in 1723. Because of this, they claim to be the oldest permanent village in Missouri. However, some people say that, since the little town's inhabitants fled the place for a short time when Indians attacked, the settlement was not permanent. Other people argue that not everyone left and the settlement really has been permanent.

On January 3, 1735, the village of Ste. Genevieve was founded by French trappers and miners. French settlers had been living in the area for three years prior to that. They did move the village once to get away from the flooding of the Mississippi River but did not leave. Because of this it is regarded by most as Missouri's oldest permanent settlement.

FIRST GERMAN IMMIGRANTS:

It was a cold January 1, 1800 when the first German-speaking immigrants came to Missouri. Twenty families crossed the frozen Mississippi River in their wagons and built their homes in what is now a part of Cape Girardeau.

FIRST SCHOOLS, CHURCHES & INSTITUTIONS:

FIRST CHURCH:

We don't have an exact date for the founding of Missouri's first church but we know it was the Catholic Church in Ste. Genevieve in about 1753. We also know that later that same year it had to be moved to higher ground because of repeated flooding. The first Catholic church was dedicated in St. Louis on June 24, 1770. It was a log structure which stood where the Old Cathedral stands today. (under the arch) Father Meurin from Ste. Genevieve started that first church in St. Louis.

FIRST WEDDING:

Father Sebastian Meurin mentioned above performed the first Christian marriage in this part of the world. On April 20, 1766, the first wedding took place in St. Louis. Canadian fur trapper, Toussain Hunaud married Marie Boujenou. The wedding took place at her house.

FIRST PROTESTANT SERMON:

John Clark from Scotland preached the first Protestant sermon in Missouri in 1798. The site of the church service was the riverbank near present day Herculaneum.

FIRST CHURCH IN ST. CHARLES:

A new church in Les Petites Cotes (Village of the Little Hills) was named San Carlos Borremeo on November 7, 1791. The village around the church changed its name on this day also. It was named for the church and called San Carlos de

Misury. In 1803 the settlement's name was changed to the "American" name, St. Charles.

FIRST PROTESTANT MARRIAGE:

On January 9, 1806 – John Clark conducted the first Protestant marriage in Missouri.

FIRST NEWSPAPER:

Meriwether Lewis brought Irish immigrant, Joseph Charless to St. Louis on July 1, 1808. On July 12, 1808, Charless published the first newspaper west of the Mississippi, *The Missouri Gazette*.

FIRST BAPTIST CHURCH IN MISSOURI:

Bethel Baptist Church was established near Jackson, MO on July 19, 1806. It was Missouri's first Baptist Church. The original log church just outside Jackson collapsed and was deteriorating when the Baptist Association came to the rescue. The old log building has been restored and now stands under a pavilion roof at its original location.

The Rev. John Mason Peck and James E. Welch organized the First Baptist Church of St. Louis on December 18, 1818. The eleven members constructed the first Protestant house of worship in St. Louis at what is now the Arch Grounds.

FIRST MASONIC LODGE:

The first Masonic Lodge in Missouri was founded at Ste. Genevieve on July 17, 1807.

FIRST PRESBYTERIAN CHURCH IN MISSOURI:

The first Presbyterian church in Missouri was organized near Potosi on August 12, 1816. The first regularly organized Presbyterian church in St. Louis with nine members in its congregation and led by Rev. Salmon Giddings was founded on

November 23, 1817. Within ten years it was up to 90 which was a lot for such a small settlement. It was the first Protestant church in St. Louis. A building for the new Presbyterian Church wasn't completed until 1826.

FIRST BANK:

On December 13, 1816, the Bank of St. Louis (the first in Missouri) opened. Bickering directors closed it three years later.

FIRST CHRISTIAN (DENOMINATION) CHURCH IN MISSOURI:

The first Christian Church in Missouri was organized in Howard County on November 22, 1817.

FIRST SCHOOL FOR GIRLS:

In St. Charles on September 14, 1818, the Sisters of the Sacred Heart founded their first school for girls in Missouri. This order was led by Saint Rose Philippine Duchesne.

FIRST EPISCOPAL CHURCH:

Colonel Thomas Fiveash Riddick was an influential banker who helped create the St. Louis public schools, was a founder of the Thespian Society and was a delegate to the original Missouri Constitutional Congress. On November 1, 1819 he founded the first Episcopal Church west of the Mississippi.

FIRST NEWSPAPER WEST OF ST. LOUIS:

On April 23, 1819, the newspaper, *Missouri Intelligencer and Boonslick Advertiser* became the first to be printed west of St. Louis. This was important because of the town's (Franklin's) place near the head of the Santa Fe Trail.

FIRST METHODIST CHURCH:

The very first permanent group of Methodists organized in St. Louis on January 7, 1821 under the leadership of Jesse Walker.

FIRST SCHOOL FOR NATIVE AMERICANS

On August 13, 1821, the Harmony Mission was established as the first school for Native American children in Missouri. It was in what is now Bates County. It ended without harmony as the mountain men, missionaries, and Native Americans could not trust each other. Another school for Native Americans was established in what is now Valley Park, MO but the building and all records have been lost.

FIRST ADVANCED SCHOOL FOR NATIVE AMERICANS:

St. Regis Seminary opened was the first Roman Catholic institution in America to be founded for the higher education of Native Americans. It opened on May 11, 1824.

FIRST MASONIC LODGE:

Missouri Royal Arch Chapter #1 of the order of Masons was organized on October 30, 1821.

THE FIRST SCHOOLS AND CHURCHES IN SPRINGFIELD:

The Methodist Conference in Cape Girardeau met and selected a young circuit rider, James H. Slavens, to start the first church of any kind in Springfield. On his way to Springfield he met the covered wagon of Joseph Rountree who was on his way there to start the very first school.

On January16, 1831, with 18" of snow on the ground, the Robert Rountree family with their son, Joseph Rountree arrived in Greene County, Missouri. During that same year, he and his pioneer friends built a crude log school house; and soon thereafter formal education began in Greene County. According to one biographer, Joseph Rountree served as teacher in the school for "two sessions." Today's Rountree School and the Rountree Neighborhood are named for them.

James Slavens preached the first sermon ever delivered in Springfield on October 10, 1831 at the home of William Fulbright on West Walnut Street. The Fullbright children were also some of the first to attend Mr. Rountree's new school.

FIRST GERMAN NEWSPAPER:

Anzeiger des Westens, the first German newspaper in Missouri was established on October 31, 1835.

FIRST MAGAZINE:

The Catholic Cabinet and Chronicle of Religious Intelligence was the catchy name of the first magazine published in Missouri in May of 1843.

FIRST STATE MEDICAL ASSOCIATION:

The State Medical Association was organized on November 4, 1850.

FIRST JEWISH CONGRETATION:

The first Jewish congregation in Missouri met in St. Louis on New Year's Day, 1836.

FIRST PUBLIC SCHOOL:

The first public school was established on April 2, 1838 by the state Legislature. While it was public and had state backing, it was not free. At least they waited a day so it wasn't on April Fool's Day.

FIRST PUBLIC LIBRARY:

On April 19, 1846, the Mercantile Library opened in St. Louis on this date thus becoming the first public library west of the Mississippi.

FIRST BASEBALL FARM SYSTEM

Born on St. Patrick's Day, 1851, in County Clare, Ireland, Timothy "Ted" Sullivan attended St. Louis U. and then managed the St. Louis Maroons professional baseball team in 1884. They finished with a 94-19 record. He went on to manage the Kansas City Cowboys where he started the nation's first "farm system" for developing players. He also described the Missourians as "fanatical" about baseball and was the first to refer to the people as "fans."

FIRST CONGREGATIONAL (DENOMINATION) CHURCH:

Missouri's first Congregational church was organized in St. Louis on March 18, 1852. A century later the Congregational Church merged with the Evangelical Reformed Churches in German communities all along Missouri's rivers. The new denomination is now known as the United Church of Christ.

THE FIRST FAIRS:

The very first state fair opened in Boonville on October 3, 1853. State fairs were held in Boonville until 1901. They have been in Sedalia ever since.

The very first Southeast Missouri District Fair was underway at Cape Girardeau on October 3, 1855. It has continued annually ever since.

Greene County had its first big fair on October 1, 1856. The Southwest Missouri Fair lasted three days and drew people from many surrounding counties. Many visitors stayed for the entire event and brought tents for the evenings. Some even brought their servants. Today the event is called the Ozark Empire Fair.

The Valley Fair was first held on October 13, 1856. It was the first fair to be held in St. Louis.

Life was rough in Platte County during the years of the Civil War so the Platte County Fair was not held in 1861 and 1862. It has been held every other year, however, from October 21, 1858 to the present.

FIRST HIGH SCHOOLS:

The first high school classes west of the Mississippi began on February 4, 1853 at the Wayman School in St. Louis.

Classes began on March 24, 1856 at the first actual high school building west of the Mississippi. (Central High in St. Louis)

AMERICA'S FIRST TEACHERS ORGANIZATION:

The nation's first organization for teachers, the Missouri State Teachers Association was founded in Columbia on May 21, 1856.

FIRST PUBLIC KINDERGARTEN:

The very first public kindergarten in America was established by Susan Elizabeth Blow in the Des Peres School in Carondolet in 1873.

FIRST Y.M.C.A.

The Y.M.C.A. was founded in St. Louis on November 4, 1875.

FIRST ART MUSEUM:

Washington University established the first Art Museum west of the Mississippi on May 10, 1881.

FIRST RURAL MAIL DELIVERY:

The first Missouri rural mail routes were established from Cairo, MO in Randolph County on October 15, 1896. Prior to that, postal patrons would go by the nearest post office from time to time and collect their mail.

FIRST HIBERNIANS:

On October 5, 1898, the Ancient Order of Hibernians was chartered in St. Louis. Their goal was to improve the lives of Irish-Americans and to help the Irish who wanted to immigrate to Missouri.

FIRST SCHOOL FOR JOURNALISTS:

On this date the School of Journalism was founded at the University of Missouri on September 14, 1908. It was the very first "J-school" in the world.

FIRST FARM BUREAU:

First Missouri Farm Bureau organized at Cape Girardeau on the first of August, 1912.

FIRST WOMEN'S CATHOLIC COLLEGE:

The cornerstone was laid for the first women's Catholic college west of the Mississippi on November 1, 1915. Loretto College started with five students. Today it is called Webster University.

FIRST CARDINAL OF THE CATHOLIC CHURCH:

Cardinal John Glennon was appointed to his high office on December 23, 1945. Thus he became the first Cardinal west of the Mississippi. On his way home from Rome he stopped in his native Ireland where he became ill and died.

FIRST HOLIDAY OBSERVANCES:

INDEPENDENCE DAY:

On July 4, 1804, Lewis and Clark marked the 28th anniversary of the birth of the nation with a discharge of the cannon at sunrise and another at sunset. They made an amazing fifteen miles progress upriver and the men were given an extra portion of whiskey in celebration of the day. They were near present day Rushville, MO. This was the first Independence Day celebration west of the Mississippi.

ST. PATRICK'S DAY:

It was early morning on March 17, 1820 when the riverboat *Shamrock* fired a salvo inviting everyone in St. Louis to the very first St. Patrick's Day celebration and parade in St. Louis and maybe the first of any community in Missouri. Now they're wearin' the green in St. Louis, Kansas City, Rolla, Saint Patrick, New Haven, Shamrock, and of course in our Irish Wilderness.

THANKSGIVING DAY:

November 30, 1843 – Thanksgiving was officially observed for the first time in Missouri on November 30, 1843. Governor Reynolds declared that the last Thursday in November should be set aside for a day of prayer and celebration.

STEAMBOAT FIRSTS:

FIRST UP THE MISSISSIPPI:

The very first steamboat reached St. Louis on August 2, 1817. Fittingly, it was the *Zebulon M. Pike*. The *Constitution* was the second steamboat to ever be in St. Louis. It arrived on October 7, 1817. From this time forward for decades the St. Louis levee would be crowded with steamboats.

FIRST UP THE MISSOURI:

The first steamboat (the *Independence*) to make it into the Missouri River arrived at St. Charles on May 13, 1819. The *Independence* is pictured on the city's seal. On May 15th, it left St. Charles for points upstream. It arrived at Franklin, MO on May 28. Most riverboats could not traverse the Missouri because of the strong current and the extreme number of submerged snags. The Independence set the pattern for future boats on the Missouri with its more shallow draft, more powerful engines and its weight and paddles shifted forward.

FIRST EXPLORATION STEAMBOAT:

On June 9, 1819, The *Western Engineer* arrived in St. Louis. A most unusual boat! Called "Long's Dragon," it was built to travel up the Missouri and it was shaped and painted to resemble a huge serpent. Smoke and steam came from its mouth and nostrils. Intended to intimidate the Native Americans, it did that very well. It left St. Louis on June 21, headed upstream to Franklin and beyond.

Loaded with scientists, a small military detachment, cannon, howitzers, and all provisions, the *Western Engineer* arrived at Franklin, MO on November 13, 1819.

177 years later a group of researchers was busy recording the tales of Shoshone Indians from their oral history. They were told of a day when a hunting party encountered a roaring serpent on the Missouri River which carried a cabin and white men on its back. Without a doubt, these men had seen the *Western Engineer* and were intimidated.

STEAMBOAT SINKINGS:

The steamboat, *Chariton*, sank at the mouth of the Gasconade and was raised, sank at Independence and was raised, blew her boiler in St. Louis killing twelve and was repaired, then sank in Euphrasie Bend near Glasgow on October 12, 1837. This was pretty typical in the life of a steamboat. They usually lasted from 3 to 5 years. You will find much more about steamboat and their related disasters in later sections of this book.

FERRIES:

Many important steamboats were ferry boats carrying passengers, livestock, and goods across our great rivers. An example of how busy they were can be seen at the ferry landing in St. Joseph.

On June 15, 1849 the Gold Rush was on and in the ten weeks prior to this date the steam-powered ferry at St. Joseph carried 1,508 wagons and averaging four men to a wagon. That would make 6,032 passengers. At Duncan's ferry, four miles above St. Joseph, 685 wagons crossed. At Bontown and Savannah, the ferries could be seen as far as the Bluffs – that's 2,000 ferries. This is a total of 4,193 wagons. About 10,000 crossed at Independence, making a total of 27,000 persons. There were about eight mules or oxen to each wagon, giving a total of 37,544 head of stock!

FIRST RAILROAD LOCOMOTIVES UP THE MISSOURI:

On June 6, 1857 the steamboat, *Delaware*, was making its way up the Missouri carrying two railroad locomotives. (the Buchanan and the St. Joseph) This was a first time for railroad engines to be engaged in river travel. Why didn't they just drive the trains up the railroad tracks to wherever they were going? Those locomotives were being taken to St. Joseph so the Hannibal-St. Joseph R.R. could be built from both ends of the state and meet in the middle.

FIRST STEAMBOATS OF WAR:

James Eads delivered his first ironclad gunboat to the Union Navy on October 12, 1861. Built in his naval yard in Carondelet, it was christened the *St. Louis*. (Some claim the *Baron DeKalb* was the first.)

FIRST HOSPITAL SHIP:

June 11, 1862 was a significant day. This is when the Cape Girardeau built, *Red Rover* accepted its first patient. It was America's first hospital ship. On Christmas Eve of 1863 several nuns were transferred from the Army hospital at Mound City, MO to the hospital ship, *Red Rover*.

They became the first women to serve aboard a Navy ship and thus, were the forerunners of the Navy Nurse Corps, the W.A.V.ES., and today's modern women of the Navy.

DUELS AND DUELING:

Dueling was a matter of settling disputes in what was considered an honorable way. Of course it was always illegal so the parties would usually agree to meet on some island in the Mississippi River and considered themselves free from any laws. Our first U.S. Senator, Thomas Hart Benton may have fought more duels than any other person. In fact he was in Missouri after fleeing from Tennessee where he was involved in a shooting and stabbing. Our first Congressman, John Scott from Ste. Genevieve, was a brilliant lawyer and debater, but he did have a temper. One morning he challenged five different men to duels.

An interesting aspect of dueling was the duty of the "second." Each person chose the man he wanted as a second. Then this man was to try everything possible to avoid having the duel take place but let each principal still retain his honor. One man could withdraw his challenge, they could agree to shoot into the air or from a great distance and miss on purpose. Just about anything was acceptable to avoid the actual confrontation. But sometimes pride or tempers got in the way and the duel went on as scheduled. Following are some of the more famous duels.

At Moreau's Island below Ste. Genevieve, Dr. Walter Fenwick and Thomas T. Crittenden fought a duel on October 1, 1811.

On August 12, 1817 Charles Lucas and Thomas Hart Benton agreed to their first duel on Bloody Island. On August 16, 1817 the two lawyers met for their first duel. At 30 paces both men were wounded.

Prominent St. Louis citizens Joshua Barton (first Missouri Secretary of State) and Thomas C. Rector fought a duel at Bloody Island on June 30, 1823. Barton was killed in the duel and Rector was unhurt. However, Rector was later killed in a knife fight.

DUELS AND DUELING: (Continued)

The final duel was fought between Thomas Hart Benton and Charles Lucas on Bloody Island September 27, 1817. Lucas was hit and said, "Colonel, you have murdered me and I never can forgive you." He died on the spot.

On September 28, 1817, while discussing the previous day's duel between Charles Lucas and Thomas Hart Benton, William Tharp pulled a pistol and killed William Smith, a St. Louis Banker.

Near New Madrid, on September 1, 1824, prominent citizens Abiel Leonard and Major Taylor Berry fought a duel on a Mississippi River Island.

On July 9, 1831, Major Thomas Biddle horsewhipped Congressman Spencer Pettis because Pettis had criticized the Bank of the United States and Biddle's brother was the bank's president. As a result, on August 26, 1831 these leading St. Louis citizens fought a duel on Bloody Island. They fired at just five feet and both were killed.

On September 22, 1842, James Shields and Abraham Lincoln came to Missouri for a duel. Shields, an Illinois attorney and State Auditor accused Lincoln of writing a newspaper article critical of him. Lincoln was the one who had been challenged so he got to choose the weapons. He chose cavalry sabers but Lincoln convinced Shields that he did not write the article so the duel was called off. Shields probably also noticed that Lincoln's long arms gave him a much longer reach.

Reformer and Editor of the St. Louis Democrat, Benjamin Gratz Brown, and District Attorney, Thomas C. Reynolds, fought a duel on Bloody Island on August 26, 1856. Brown was wounded and Reynolds was unhurt. Brown went on to become Governor of Missouri and Reynolds went on to become the Confederate Governor of Missouri.

DUELS AND DUELING: (Continued)

The Marmaduke-Walker Duel took place on September 6, 1863. While this duel was fought in Arkansas, it featured General John Sappington Marmaduke (a Missouri Governor) who was under the command of General Sterling Price (another Missouri Governor.) Marmaduke won by killing another General, Lucius M. Walker.

So what became of dueling? Of course it was always illegal so it wasn't the laws that made it go away. Some claim that Wild Bill Hickok made formal dueling disappear when he modified the practice in Springfield, Missouri one day in 1865. Hickok is said to have turned it into the historic Wild West quick draw version of dueling. You will read about this shortly.

LAWS, LAW ENFORCEMENT, AND

PUBLIC SAFETY:

FIRST LEGISLATURE:

Missouri's very first legislature met on June 11, 1806 in St. Louis with a total of four members. Of course this was a territorial legislature.

FIRST POLICE ORDINANCE:

The first ordinance in St. Louis concerning public safety was passed on December 23, 1809. There were no policemen but every man over the age of 18 was required to enforce the laws.

FIRST REPRESENTATIVE GOVERNMENT:

On December 7, 1812, the newly elected House of Representatives of the first territorial General Assembly met at the home of Joseph Robidoux in St. Louis. This was the first act of representative government in Missouri. (And our first capital?)

FIRST LOTTERY:

On January 28, 1817, Governor William Clark authorized a territorial lottery. It was to use profits to purchase fire equipment for the territory's capital city. (St. Louis) But Missourians hated lotteries and would not buy tickets.

THE FIRST STATE CONSTITUTION:

At the temporary capital in St. Louis Missouri's first Constitution was adopted on July 19, 1820.

FIRST ELECTIONS:

Our first statewide elections were held on August 28, 1820. We had applied for statehood but not yet been accepted into the Union. Alexander McNair was elected Governor.

FIRST GENERAL ASSEMBLY:

The full General Assembly met for the first time on September 18, 1820. They met in the Missouri Hotel in St. Louis. (So, would that be our first or second capital building?)

FIRST WRITTEN BALLOTS:

St. Louis decreed on December 17, 1822, that written ballots rather than oral voting was officially required now for all city elections. Prior to this, a voter was required to step before the poll watchers and loudly announce his vote. This was to allow all concerned to keep an accurate account. The secret ballot would first be used in Australia. When it was implemented here, many called it the "Australian Ballot." See George Caleb Bingham's painting, "The County Election."

FIRST WRITTEN BALLOTS:

Haven't we already done this? Yes, back in 1822 they were required but they didn't actually obey the law for 20 years! On December 17, 1842 voting in St. Louis was actually done for the first time with paper ballots rather than by a voice vote.

FIRST FORMAL POLICE FORCE:

Back in 1809 all men in St. Louis were required to enforce the laws. Finally, on February 23, 1826, the city of St, Louis passed an ordinance providing for a real police force of 27 men. The problem is that it took twenty years to actually organize the force.

FIRST PERMANENT STATE CAPITAL:

Until November 20, 1826, the State Legislature had met in St. Louis or St. Charles. On this day they met for the first time in Jefferson City. (Our fourth capital building?)

FIRST STATE PENITENTIARY:

On March 1, 1836, the state's first penitentiary at Jefferson City was opened. Designed for 40 prisoners, it already had 46 on opening day. Its first prisoner, a burglar from Greene County.

FIRST FIRE ENGINE:

St. Louis purchased its first steam-powered fire engine on August 1, 1854. Prior to that, water was pumped to the hoses by men with large hand pumps. On December 26, 1855 that first steam fire engine arrived and was dragged across the frozen Mississippi by a team of horses and taken to the fire station.

SLAVERY ABOLISHED:

On January 11, 1865, Missouri abolished slavery and became the first former slave state to do so.

FIRST MOUNTED POLICE:

The Mounted police in St. Louis and Kansas City are extremely effective in patrolling and controlling crowds. Their long tradition began in St. Louis on March 13, 1867 when they were first established.

FIRST GOVERNOR IN THE MANSION:

On January 20, 1872 Governor B. Gratz Brown and his family become the first to occupy the new Governor's Mansion.

FIRSTS FOR PHOEBE COUZINS:

FIRST LAW SCHOOL GRADUATE:

Phoebe Couzins was born in St. Louis on September 8, 1842. On May 8, 1871, she became Missouri's first woman law school graduate. (Washington University in St. Louis).

FIRST FEMALE MARSHALL:

In 1887, Phoebe Couzins became the first female US Marshall in the country's history. She was also on the Board of Directors for the World's Fair.

FIRST FEMALE ATTORNEY:

Couzins became the first woman attorney in Missouri's history. She was best known for her powerful speeches for women's suffrage and for prohibition. In 1887, she switched positions and began to work against the vote for women and against the prohibition movement. This remarkable woman died in abject poverty on December 5, 1913.

FIRST WILD WEST SHOOTOUT:

William Hickok, also known as Wild Bill, already had a reputation by October 27, 1862. That is when he was attending a band concert at the Kansas City Exposition. About 50 drunken Texas drovers were also there and insisted that the band play Dixie. Hickok told the band to go on with the concert and found 50 pistols pointed at him. Somehow he made the Texans back down.

Then, on July 21, 1865, Hickok found himself being tormented by Davis Tutt and Tutt's companions in downtown Springfield. That day, Hickok killed Davis Tutt in what some cite as the first true western showdown.

Wild Bill left Missouri immediately after that gunfight but we know that he returned. There are records of him serving as an umpire for professional baseball in Kansas City.

On August 12, 1866, Wild Bill Hickok umpired the baseball game between a rival team from Atchison, KS and the Kansas City Antelopes. The Antelopes won 48 to 28. And yes, Wild Bill did wear both six-guns while he called balls and strikes so there were no arguments.

William 'Wild Bill'
Hickok

THE JAMES GANG:

September 5, 1847 was the birthday of an expert on Missouri law, military affairs, and railroad and bank withdrawals; Jesse James. He was born in Clay County, MO. This man and his companions are a true enigma to historians. Considered by many to be a lowly outlaw, others considered him to be a champion fighting for justice. Some thought of him as a latter day Robin Hood. And how did he and his close friends have so many people in high offices looking after their interests? Was he just the public face of a much larger and secretive group? He was certainly one of the most interesting characters in our history.

FIRST BANK ROBBERY:

On February 13, 1866, Jesse James & Co. pulled off their first bank robbery. It was near his home at Liberty, MO. He held up many other banks over the years and received accolades from the public and press whenever he did so. His targets were usually the banks, the railroads, and the Army. These were the three entities responsible for much of the suffering among his family and friends.

Other notable bank robberies included May 27, 1873 hold-up of the bank at Ste. Genevieve and hitting the "un-robbable bank" at Gallatin. At Gallatin the gang shot a teller who they claimed had killed their fellow soldier, William Anderson. People in Northfield, Minnesota had been warned in advance and were waiting when the James gang entered the bank. Only Jesse and his brother Frank escaped alive that day.

FIRST TRAIN ROBBERY:

Of course no one could rob a train. They're big, fast-moving, and well-protected. Near Gads Hill, the James gang robbed their first train on January 31, 1874. After the robbery, Jesse gave the conductor a written press release so the information would be reported accurately.

On September 8, 1874, reports were printed in St. Louis about a train robbery that didn't happen. It seems that the Lexington Band was returning home from a week of playing at a fair and had their pay with them. The band feared a holdup so they armed themselves. The James gang stopped the train but, seeing so many armed men, decided to leave.

The story says that Jesse was shot in the back by one of his own men while straightening a picture at his home in St. Joseph. Some forensic researchers' claim that was not Jesse. At any rate, Jesse disappeared from public view and was presumed dead.

Finally, after having robbed dozens of banks and trains over nearly two decades, Frank James finally turned himself in October, 1882. He surrendered by meeting the Governor on the steps of the Capital Building and making a short but eloquent speech. Then handing his gun to the Governor himself.

His trial began on August 21, 1883 in Gallatin and was held at the City Opera House to accommodate the large crowds of spectators. James had a team of eight attorneys including a former Lieutenant Governor and the President of the Bar Association of Missouri. On September 6 he was found Not Guilty of the crime. In fact, he was never convicted of any crime in Missouri.

FIRST TRAIN ROBBERY: (Continued)

If Jesse James was still alive as an old man, he lived in obscurity for his final years. Frank worked at many jobs including managing the race tracks for the state of Louisiana, starring in a wild-west show and working as a bouncer in a St. Louis Theater.

On June 28, 1902, Frank announced that Frank James had decided to live again in Kearny, MO along with his wife. He also stated (through his attorney) that his aged mother was planning to live with them. To make the family complete again, the body of Jesse James would be moved from its grave of 20 years. Every rig in Kearny and Excelsior Springs was rented out for the day so people could watch the procession.

FIRST K.C. POLICE OFFICER KILLED:

On New Year's Eve, 1881 in the White House Saloon, a drunkard killed Officer Martin Hayes. This was the first time a Kansas City police officer had been killed in the line of duty.

FIRST HORSELESS CARRIAGE:

St. Louis' (and Missouri's?) first horseless carriage appeared on April 14, 1893. 20-year-old Perry Lewis built the electric car that would go ten mph. It would be another five years before an internal combustion carriage would appear in St. Louis.

FIRST CRACKDOWN ON BICYCLES:

St. Louis police launched a crackdown on bicycle "scorching" and "reckless wheeling" and violators were to be charged with "felonious wounding" if they injured any pedestrians. The date was September 5, 1896.

FIRST WOMAN LEGALLY WEARS PANTS ON THE JOB:

A female housepainter in St. Louis asked the city for permission to wear trousers while she climbed the ladders at work. Permission was granted on January 15, 1902.

FIRST LICENSE PLATES:

On March 23, 1903, automobile license plates came to Missouri. The same legislation set a state speed limit of nine miles per hour and required automobiles to sound a horn or a bell before passing a horse-drawn vehicle.

FIRST USE OF FINGERPRINTS BY POLICE:

The St. Louis police department became the first in the nation to use fingerprints for identification on August 1, 1904.

FIRST FINGERPRINT EXCHANGE:

Police departments in St. Louis and in London, England became the first anywhere to exchange fingerprints between Europe and America On July 6, 1905.

FIRST VEHICULAR MANSLAUGHTER:

On February 14, 1908, a chauffeur became the first driver in Missouri convicted of manslaughter for killing a pedestrian.

FIRST FIRE TRUCK WRECK:

It was on February 20, 1908 that St. Louis' first automobile fire truck was rushing to a fire on this date and rounded a corner at 50 mph, struck a curb, and threw seven men from the truck.

FIRST CHASE CAR:

Constable George Bode became the first lawman in a rural area of Missouri (Clayton) to obtain a chase car to catch the "scorchers" who were speeding through his town. On December 5, 1908 he threatened to mount two repeating rifles on his chase car if needed.

FIRST WOMAN TO VOTE:

On August 31, 1920 Marie Byrum became the first woman to vote in the state's history.

FIRST WOMAN ELECTED MAYOR:

The citizens of St. James elected Mayme Ousley to be the first woman mayor in the state. This was on April 5, 1921 and just two years after women won the right to vote. The honorable Mrs. Ousley was famous for beautifying the public spaces in St. James. At the edges of the town she had signs erected which stated, *"Drive slow and see our beautiful city, drive fast and see our jail."*

FIRST FEMALE LAWMAKERS:

Mellcene Smith and Lucille Turner became the first women *elected to the State Legislature on November 7, 1922.*

TRIVIA: As one visits our state capitol building, it's interesting to notice all of the beautiful old brass drinking fountains. They are very tall! This is because the politicians and architects of that time could not imagine women ever having offices in that building. Neither could they imagine thousands of students there daily on field trips.

FIRST RADIO PATROL CARS:

The St. Louis police got their first radios in the patrol cars on July 22, 1930.

FIRST HIGHWAY PATROL:

The law creating the Missouri State Highway Patrol went into effect on September 14, 1931. While waiting for the big day the state had acquired 49 troopers, 36 new Ford Model A roadsters, a Ford sedan, a Plymouth sedan, a Buick, three Chevys and twelve Harleys.

FIRST STATE TROOPER KILLED:

On June 14, 1933 Sergeant Benjamin Booth was killed along with a Boone County sheriff in Columbia. This was the result of a shootout with bank robbers. Booth was the first State Trooper to die in the line of duty.

FIRST HIGHWAY PATROL AIRCRAFT:

On August 28, 1946, two war surplus single-engine aircraft were purchased as the state's first Highway Patrol airplanes.

FIRST AFRICAN-AMERICAN SENATOR:

Theodore D. McNeal was elected the first black Senator in Missouri on November 8, 1960.

FIRST WOMAN IN STATEWIDE OFFICE:

On May 30, 1984, Margaret B. Kelly became the first woman to hold a state-wide office in Missouri. She was not elected but appointed to be State Auditor.

SPORTS FIRSTS:

FIRST PROFESSIONAL BASEBALL GAME:

To test the market for professional baseball, a team of professional players played an amateur all-star team in St. Louis on March 27, 1875. The "Pros" won 15 to 0. One thousand people attended the game. The next year the city got a pro team.

FIRST NATIONAL LEAGUE GAME:

On May 4, 1876 the first National League game took place in Missouri. The Brown Stockings (later called the Cardinals) played the Chicago White Stockings. They had played before in the National Association but this was a whole new league. That first game was rained out in the 3rd.

FIRST BASEBALL FARM SYSTEM

Timothy "Ted" Sullivan was born in County Clare, Ireland. He attended St. Louis U. and then managed the St. Louis Maroons professional baseball team in 1884. They finished with a 94-19 record. He went on to manage the Kansas City Cowboys where he started the nation's first "farm system" for developing players. He also described the Missourians as "fanatical" about baseball and was the first to refer to the people as "fans."

FIRST PRO BASEBALL IN KANSAS CITY:

Professional baseball came to Kansas City for the first time on a cold February 9, 1886. The team was the American League's "Kansas City Cowboys." The team's starting pitcher, **Stump Wiedman,** set a record by losing 36 games that year. They played their first game on April 30, 1886. Their opponent was the Chicago White Stockings.

Other teams in the league with K.C. included the St. Louis Maroons and the Boston Beaneaters. The only team the Cowboys could routinely beat that year was the Washington Senators.

FIRST MIZZOU FOOTBALL:

The University of Missouri played its first football game against another school – Washington University in St. Louis on November 27, 1890.

FIRST WOMAN CYCLING CHAMP:

On September 1, 1894, Minnie Walden, a "pretty blonde of 18," became the first woman to win a bicycle race in the United States. The one mile race through North St. Louis garnered two prizes, a sweater and a diamond ring.

FIRST FORWARD PASS IN FOOTBALL:

Bradbury Robinson of St. Louis University threw the first legal forward pass in football on September 5, 1906. Perfecting the pass caused them to outscore their opponents that season by 402-11.

1905 had been a bloody year in college football. 18 players had been killed and 159 seriously injured. There were moves to abolish the game. But President **Theodore Roosevelt** personally intervened and demanded that the rules of the game be reformed thinking it would be safer to pass the ball.

FIRST MIZZOU vs. KANSAS BASKETBALL GAME:

The University of Missouri Tigers met the Kansas Jayhawks basketball team for the first time on March 11, 1907. Missouri won 34-32. They played again the very next day and Missouri won 34-12.

FIRST WOMEN'S BOWLING TOURNAMENT:

America's very first bowling tournament exclusively for women began in St Louis on March 17, 1917.

FIRST BIRDS ON THE BAT:

On April 8, 1922, the Cardinals played the Browns and showed off their new uniforms. For the first time they had two birds on a bat with "*Cardinals*" underneath.

FIRST NUMBERS ON BASEBALL UNIFORMS:

It was March 6, 1923 when the Cardinals came up with a new idea. Players would begin wearing numbers on their uniforms. Years later, it would be the Cardinals again who would start putting player's names on the uniforms.

FIRST K.C. PRO FOOTBALL TEAM:

On January 26, 1924, the National Football League franchised the team farthest west of all their teams, the Kansas City Blues. But the people in Kansas City didn't get to see any of the games. The Blues had to play all of their games on the road because the other teams all refused to travel that far west.

FIRST "COLORED WORLD SERIES"

The first "Colored World Series" got underway on October 20, 1924 in Kansas City.   It featured the K.C. Monarchs and the Hillsdale (Philadelphia) Daisies. KC won the 9-game series: 5 games to 4 with one tie.

FIRST TELEVISED SPORTING EVENT:

The first sporting event televised in Missouri took place on February 14, 1947. The basketball game between Oklahoma and St. Louis U. was televised by KSD-TV.

FIRST TELEVISED GOLF:

The U.S. Open was played at St. Louis Country Club and televised on KSD-TV on June 15, 1947. It was the first televised golf match in the nation.

FIRST HOME OPENER NIGHT GAME:

For the first time in baseball history an opening day game was played at night when the Cardinals beat the Pirates under the lights in St. Louis on April 17, 1950.

FIRST DAY FOR KANSAS CITY A's

On November 8, 1954, the American League approved the transfer of Philadelphia's Athletics to Kansas City. They played their first game on April 12, 1955.

FIRST NIGHT OF WRESTLING AT THE CHASE:

Admitting that professional wrestling may not be a sport, we will note that "Wrestling at the Chase" in St. Louis began its 24-year run on television on May 23, 1959.

FIRST SUPER BOWL:

On January 15, 1967, the Kansas City Chiefs appeared in the nation's very first Super Bowl.

FIRST GAME FOR K.C. ROYALS:

The first game of the Kansas City Royals was on April 8, 1969.

FIRST GAME AT ARROWHEAD:

The very first football game was played at the wonderful Arrowhead Stadium on September 17, 1972.

FIRST GAME FOR THE K.C. KINGS:

The first game of the NBA Kansas City Kings was November 10, 1974.

FIRST MAN AROUND THE WORLD IN A BALLOON:

From June 19, 2002 - July 3, 2002 Steve Fossett circumnavigated the globe in 13 days, 8 hours, 33 minutes (14 days, 19 hours, 50 minutes to landing) and 20,626.48 statute miles by himself in the balloon, *Spirit of Freedom*. His home base was Washington University in St. Louis.

FIRSTS IN SCIENCE AND INVENTIONS:

FIRST SCIENTIST:

Dr. Antoine Francois Saugrain de Vigne was born back in 1763 and he came to St. Louis when it was still a small settlement. He was the first scientist west of the Mississippi and provided scientific equipment for Lewis and Clark. One item he gave them was matches which were not in use yet in other parts of the country.

FIRST WEATHER MAN:

Dr. George Engelmann began taking weather readings in St. Louis on New Year's Day, 1836. His 47 years of records are the only ones we have for that period. He was also largely responsible for developing Henry Shaw's garden.

FIRST GAS STREET LIGHTS:

On November 3, 1847, St. Louis was illuminated with gas lights.

FIRST TELEGRAPH:

On December 20, 1847, St. Louis was connected to the East by telegraph. The very first telegraph was sent to St. Louis the following day. It was sent to the _Missouri Republican_ newspaper from Louisville.

FIRST LONG-DISTANCE TELEPHONE:

Long distance telephone service began in Missouri on December 18, 1877. The first line ran between Jackson and Cape Girardeau. St. Louis-Hannibal and Columbia-Rocheport were connected later that same year.

FIRST TELEPHONE SERVICE:

It was April 19, 1878 when telephone service came to St. Louis for the first time. The new phone company had twelve original customers. It also came to Hannibal in 1878.

FIRST ELECTRIC LIGHTS IN A PUBLIC BUILDINGS:

Tony Faust's Restaurant in St. Louis became the first building in Missouri to be lit by electricity on October 7, 1878. This elegant restaurant, however, was small and expensive so most people couldn't appreciate the lights. That is why on April 12, 1880, St. Louis residents crowded into the Samuel Davis & Co. Dry Goods Store to see three floors illuminated by electric lights. A generator was in the basement. It was very much the same thing on March 24, 1881, when electricity was used indoors for the first time in Kansas City at the G.Y. Smith & Co. Dry Goods Store on Main Street.

FIRST CROSS-STATE LONG DISTANCE CALL:

The first cross-state long distance call was made on October 12, 1885. The mayor of Kansas City called to his home from St. Louis.

FIRST CAR PHONE:

A driver in St. Louis placed a phone call on June 17, 1946 and made history. It was from his car and therefore the first mobile telephone call in history.

FIRST DAY FOR RALSTON-PURINA:

On Christmas Eve, 1892, William Danforth opened a small feed store in St. Louis. After a tornado destroyed the building in 1896, he put up a new building. In 1902, he changed the name to Ralston-Purina Company and it became one of the world's great agricultural research and development companies.

FIRST RADIO:

At a meeting of the National Electric Light Association in St. Louis on March 1, 1893, Nikola Tesla made the first public demonstration of a new device called a radio.

FIRST ESCALATOR:

On March 9, 1904, the May Company announced a new device in their downtown St. Louis store. It was called an "Escalader" and was described as a moving staircase.

FIRST SALE OF SLICED BREAD:

This is hard to believe but true. On July 7, 1928, loaves of sliced bread were sold at a bakery for the first time in the history of the world at The Chillicothe Baking Company.

Bread could never be sliced before being sold because it would dry out too rapidly. The baker in Chillicothe, MO combined a new slicing machine with a new treated paper wrapper to make this possible. It was advertised as the greatest thing since wrapped bread. F.D.R.'s administration later outlawed sliced bread but the home-makers rebelled and won out.

FIRST "UN-COLA"

On October 12, 1929, C.L. Grigg of St. Louis introduced his new soft drink. The Howdy Soft Drink Company was pushing "Bib-Label Lithiated Lemon-Lime Soda." It sold well in spite of that name. In 1931 he changed the name to "7-Up."

FIRST AIR-CONDITIONING:

It was December 19, 1933 when The *St. Louis Globe Democrat* ran a story about a home in St. Louis County that had the first whole-house air conditioning in the area. Prior to that some folks had been "air cooling" buildings by blowing a fan over ice.

THE FIRST "NUKE"

The Nuclear Power Plant in Callaway County was declared fully operational on December 19, 1984.

FIRST T.V. IN A HOTEL:

The Hotel Statler was advertising television sets in all hotel rooms on May 24, 1949. Each set had a seven inch screen.

FIRST WIND-POWERED COMMUNITY:

The Green Switch Celebration was held on April 18, 2008 as Rock Port, MO became the first community in America to get all of its electricity from wind power.

Windmills at the Rock Port Wind Farm

FIRSTS IN RAILROADING:

FIRST RAILROAD IN MISSOURI:

Groundbreaking ceremonies were held in St. Louis for the new Pacific Railroad on July 4th, 1851. This was the first railroad to actually be built in Missouri.

FIRST RAILROAD WHISTLE:

Livestock and people on the tracks were becoming problems so loud steam whistles were being added to railroad locomotives. On May 12, 1852, a railroad whistle was blown for the first time west of the Mississippi.

FIRST RUN BY A RAILROAD LOCOMOTIVE:

On November 12, 1852, the first railroad locomotive to operate west of the Mississippi (named the Pacific) made its very first run. It went four miles west from St. Louis to the Manchester Road.

FIRST TRAIN ON THE FIRST RAILROAD:

On December 23, 1852, they hooked railroad cars to the locomotive and first train ran on the first railroad west of the Mississippi River, the Pacific Railroad of Missouri from St. Louis to Cheltenham, a distance of five miles. (Cheltenham is now known as the 'Dogtown Neighborhood' and is right across from the zoo.)

THE FIRST RAILROAD DISASTER:

On a cold and rainy day the first railroad train between St. Louis and Jefferson City fell through a bridge over the rain-swollen Gasconade River. That happened on November 1,

1855. There is much more to this story so read about it in the "Disasters" section of this book.

TRIVIA: It wasn't any sort of first and it wasn't in Missouri but it was a terribly important day on April 21, 1856 when a railroad bridge opened between Davenport, IA, and Rock Island, IL. Since St. Louis had no railroad bridge, cross-country rail traffic shifted north. This caused the much smaller city of Chicago to start growing and eventually pass St. Louis in size.

FIRST RAILROAD ACROSS THE STATE:

The first railroad across the state was completed between Hannibal and St. Joseph. On February 13, 1859 the eastbound section was joined with the westbound section at Chillicothe. The Hannibal-St. Joe Railroad was built along the old stagecoach route known as the Hound Dog Trail.   This railroad carried the mail to St. Joseph for the Pony Express.

The first train from the east arrived in St. Joseph the very next day. Until after the Civil War, this remained the farthest point west on any railroad. By 1900 St. Joe received more than 100 passenger trains per day.

FIRST TRAIN TO KANSAS CITY:

On December 19, 1864, the Pacific Railroad reached Kansas City from St. Louis. Even before this date Kansas City was already a thriving railroad terminus. The first engines had been brought to K.C. by riverboat and they pulled trains into Kansas and westward. Passengers also would ride steamboats to K.C. and then board trains for the rest of their journey. With the Civil War closing, the rest of the track could be laid across Missouri and the East-West connection became complete.

FIRST SCHEDULED EAST-WEST SERVICE:

The first regularly scheduled train service between St. Louis and Kansas City began on October 2, 1865. It was an 18-hour trip.

FIRST MISSOURI RIVER BRIDGE:

On July 3, 1869, the Burlington Bridge at Kansas City was completed. It was the first bridge ever built across the Missouri River. The bridge was the brainchild of Kersey Coates, the developer of Quality Hill, and this bridge caused Kansas City to become the dominant city of he region rather than Leavenworth.

A RECURRING NIGHTMARE
THE BRIDGES AT ST. CHARLES:

Back in 1870 men were working hard to construct a railroad bridge across the Missouri River at St. Charles. On November 11, it collapsed killing nineteen and injuring many more. This was the first of many disasters to come.

On May 29, of 1871, they managed to get the bridge open to railroad traffic but then on May 1, 1875, the side was ripped off the *St. Luke*, a river steam boat, as it hit the St. Charles Bridge and sank.

On the 8th of November 1879, the bridge crossing the Missouri at St. Charles collapsed for the second time. Grain and livestock were thrown into the water and five men were killed. They made repairs and got the thing re-opened but then on December 8, 1881, it collapsed for the third time! Thirty one freight cars plunged into the river.

It was also proving to be a hazard for steamboats. On June 22, 1884 the riverboat *Montana* wrecked on the St. Charles Bridge.

A RECURRING NIGHTMARE
THE BRIDGES AT ST. CHARLES: (Continued)

On June 1, 1890, the first Missouri River Bridge (other than a rail bridge) was opened. This one was for pedestrians, wagons, livestock, and an occasional horseless carriage. It was a pontoon bridge that actually floated on the river at St. Charles. Does that sound like a good idea to you? The winter's ice floating downstream destroyed it five months after it opened. Pedestrians and Autos were allowed to cross the Old St. Charles Bridge for the first time on May 22, 1904.

Nature got involved when on September 20, 1916, sparks from a KATY Railroad train set fire to pigeon's nests on the old bridge. The entire wooden bridge deck was consumed in flames.

In the early 1900's, a bridge for automobiles was needed so a good one was constructed. Then, on June 25, 1935, a Wabash railway train struck a pier on the highway bridge at St. Charles. One span crashed down onto Main Street and the train crashed into the side of a hotel. No one was hurt! However, the bridge was unusable and ferry boats were put into service.

But the nightmare wasn't over yet. On May 19, 1990, the *Spirit of St. Charles* riverboat crashed into the bridge in that city. Twenty-two people were injured.

FIRST TRAIN TO SPRINGFIELD:

The first train from St. Louis reached Springfield, Missouri on April 21, 1870. This took 16 years of building because of the interruptions of the War Between the States and the terrain of the Ozark Mountains. The railroad was officially welcomed into Springfield, on May 3, 1870. This effectively removed the Ozarks as a barrier to Springfield's connection with the east. It also meant that cattle driven from the southwest could be driven to the railhead at Springfield instead of Sedalia.

Newspapers reported that "Almost everyone in the city and Greene County was there to see it." It was common for entire counties to welcome the first trains to a place.

FIRST BRIDGE AT ST. JOSEPH:

The first railroad bridge at St. Joseph opened to traffic on May 20, 1873.

FIRST DAY FOR K.C.'s UNION STATION:

Kansas City's beautiful Union Station opened for business on October 30, 1914. A few years earlier each railroad operated its own railway station. In large cities the stations would be in different parts of town. This was a huge problem for travelers needing to change trains. Then large cities began to build one large station in each city and all of the railroads shared this one "Union Station."

RAILROAD TRIVIA:

A report released on June 30, 1898, showed that at that time Missouri had 146 railroads operated by fifty-eight companies. This included mainlines and spurs but not street railroads, logging railroads and lines operated by electricity.

Of the 114 counties in Missouri, 108 of them had railroads in 1898. In the Ozarks, only Dallas, Douglas, Maries, Ozark, Stone and Taney Counties, were without a railroad. There were 1,578 railroad stations in the State, including union stations, there were four.

ROADS, STAGE COACHES & AUTOMOBILES

FIRST ROAD FROM ST. LOUIS TO SPRINGFIELD:

On February 6, 1837, the State approved a road from St. Louis to Springfield following an old Indian path, The Osage Trail. With continual improvements this morphed into the Military Road, the Wire Road, Route 66, and Interstate 44.

FIRST WAGON TRAIN FROM INDEPENDENCE:

The first wagon train left Independence, MO headed for the west coast on May Day, 1841.

FIRST LARGE WAGON TRAIN WEST:

The first large wagon train (more than 1000 people) left Independence for the Oregon Territory on May 22, 1843.

FIRST STAGE FROM INDEPENDENCE TO SANTE FE:

The first mail stage ran from Independence to Santa Fe beginning on this day July 1, 1850.

FIRST BUTTERFIELD STAGE BETWEEN MISSOURI AND CALIFORNIA:

This first stage left Tipton on September 16, 1858 and arrived in San Francisco 25 days later.

FIRST EASTBOUND MAIL FROM CALIFONIA TO ST. LOUIS:

On October 9, 1858, the first Overland Mail from California reached St. Louis. It was carried to the route terminus at Tipton, MO and put on a train for St. Louis. The trip took almost 25 days.

FIRST BUTTERFIELD STAGE – SPRINGFIELD:

The first westbound Butterfield Overland stagecoach passed through the key city of Springfield amid a tremendous celebration. It started at the Headquarters in Tipton on September 16 and reached Springfield on September 17, 1858. The first eastbound Butterfield Overland Stage passed through Springfield from San Francisco on October 22, 1858.

THE EADS BRIDGE:

While constructing the Eads Bridge, James B. Eads used something he called an "air chamber." What some call a "diving bell" allowed men to work underwater in a pocket of trapped air. On February 7, 1870, Eads hosted a champagne party for reporters under the Mississippi so they could see how it worked.

On March 19, 1870, while working below the Mississippi and building the caissons of the Eads Bridge, James Riley died. He was the first American to die of what they called Caissons Disease and we now call "the Bends".

A big crowd of onlookers cheered as a "test elephant" was led across Eads Bridge on June 14, 1874. People believed that elephants could somehow sense whether or not a structure could support its weight. Eventually Eads ran 14 locomotives back and forth across the bridge while inspectors looked for signs of stress.

The "impossible" was realized on May 23, 1874. The Eads Bridge across the Mississippi was completed and opened for pedestrians. This privately funded bridge cost five cents to cross or, for ten cents, you could stay and "promenade in the cool river breezes." On July 4, 1874, the Bridge was opened for general transportation.

FIRST BRIDGE AT JEFFERSON CITY

On May 22, 1895, a gigantic ground breaking celebration was held for the new bridge at Jefferson City. A newspaper editor said it "was enough to make Quigley wriggle."

FIRST CAR IN ST. LOUIS:

On October 20, 1897 the _Globe-Democrat_ reported that St. Louis would soon have a horseless carriage. Steel magnate Harry Scullin had ordered an electric "runabout buggy."

FIRST AUTOMOBILE MANUFACTURER IN ST. LOUIS:

There were more than 200 makes of motorcars built in St. Louis from 1890-1930. The very first automobile manufacturing company in the city was founded on May 8, 1898. The car, called a Dorris, appeared on Thanksgiving Day, 1898.

Mr. & Mrs. George Dorris in a 1901 "St. Louis"

FIRST MAYOR WITH A HORSELESS CARRIAGE:

It was July 27, 1904, when the first mayor in the U.S. to have an automobile got his new car. Mayor Rolla Wells was immediately challenged to a race with the police department's new "scorcher wagon."

FIRST GAS STATION:

C.H. Laessig opened the first gas station in the United States in 1905. It was at 418 South Teresa in St. Louis. Laessig and his partner Harry Grenner ran a garden hose from a tank to fill up the cars. Prior to that time, most motorists brought a can to a store (usually the drug store) for gasoline. Laessig and Grenner ended up with a chain of 40 stations across St. Louis.

FIRST NEWSPAPER DELIVERD BY AUTOMOBILE:

The *Post-Dispatch* became the first newspaper in the country to deliver papers by automobile on December 3, 1907.

FIRST AUTOMOBILE SHOW:

Over 20,000 people attended the first automobile show ever in St. Louis. More than 300 automobiles were on hand over the six days beginning on March 30, 1907.

THE FIRST TAXI:

The Mississippi Valley Auto Company began operating the first taxi service in Missouri on December 21, 1908. David R. Francis was the first customer riding from Newstead and Maryland (Central West End) to North 4th Street in St. Louis.

FIRST ROAD TRIP TO COLUMBIA:

W. B. West drove his automobile (Oldsmobile) from St. Louis to Columbia on June 4, 1905. He was the first person to do so. It took 14 ½ hours.

FIRST TELEPHONE IN A CAR:

On May 13, 1946, St. Louis became the first city in the nation to offer telephones in your car. A radio telephone was available for $15.00 a month.

FIRST INTERSTATE HIGHWAYS:

On August 2, 1956, Missouri became the first state to award a contract under the new Interstate Highway law. The first contract was for work on US 66 in Laclede County. Lebanon had the dubious honor of being the first town in Missouri by-passed by an Interstate highway.

FIRST DRIVE-THROUGH WINDOW:

Red Chaney invented the drive-through window in 1959. For 38 years he operated his restaurant, "Red's Giant Hamburg" on Route 66 in Springfield. Yes, he actually did run out of room on his sign and couldn't finish the word "hamburger."

FIRST SELF-PUMP GASOLINE:

On March 9, 1972, a Sinclair station in St. Louis was offering "mini service" where the station attendant pumped gas but performed no other service. This saved about 2 cents per gallon. Prior to that, gas stations were called "service stations" and would automatically check a customer's oil level, wash the windshield and check the tires' air pressure or radiator levels. At this time in Columbia some stations had started offering "self-serve" for patrons in order to get the costs lower.

FIRST ELECTRIC CAR CHARGING STATION:

The first public charging station for electric cars was opened in St. Louis on January 24, 2012. Will it be the first of many or the first of a flop? This is history in the making.

BOOKS, TV, MOVIES AND ENTERTAINMENT FIRSTS:

FIRST POEM:

Thirty-two year old Jean Baptiste Truteau was the first schoolmaster in St. Louis and is believed to have written the first poem in Missouri. It was about the attack on St. Louis in 1780 and it accused the Spanish Lieutenant Governor of cowardice.

FIRST LIVE ENTERTAINMENT:

The *Missouri Gazette* carried an advertisement for what seems to be the first live entertainment in the state's history. On January 15, 1814 a magician claimed to present a "Spectacle of 'recreative sports, of Mathematicks, and Phisicks'." Among other things, he promised to cut the head off a chicken then fix it back like new.

FIRST PLAY:

On December 31, 1814 the *Missouri Gazette* announced that a group of young men had formed a "dramatic corps" and were planning two performances that week at the courthouse. Then on January 6, 1815, Missourians saw the first theatrical production in the territory. Two plays were performed at the Courthouse in St. Louis.

FIRST PLAY WRITTEN IN MISSOURI:

On December 16, 1820 the first play written in St. Louis was performed in a makeshift theater. An officer from Jefferson Barracks wrote, *The Pedlar*, a three-act farce.

FIRST FORMAL BALL:

On February 22, 1817, Governor William Clark hosted a gala dinner – the first celebration of Washington's Birthday in Missouri. The practice was repeated every year after that in early St. Louis. The people enjoyed it so much that after 1817 they had two winter balls which occurring annually.

FIRST PERMANENT THEATER:

The first permanent theater in Missouri opened on February 1, 1819. The 600 seat theater was in the village of St. Louis.

FIRST BOOKSTORE:

In 1820 almost every store of any kind had a few books for sale. But on April 26, 1820 the *Missouri Gazette* carried an ad for an actual book store – The first in St. Louis and maybe the territory.

FIRST SECRETARY OF AGRICULTURE:

Norman Colman was born May 16, 1827. In St. Louis he published a magazine, *Colman's Rural World*. President Cleveland named Colman the nation's first Secretary of Agriculture.

FIRST HORSE RACE:

The St. Louis Jockey Club sponsored an official horse race on October 9, 1828. This was the very first one in St. Louis and maybe the first in Missouri.

FIRST THEATER:

Meriwether Lewis Clark, son of the explorer, designed a new theater for St. Louis and the cornerstone was laid on May 24, 1836. It was the first in the nation to have individual seats for the patrons. It opened on July 3, 1837. The St. Louis Theater could seat about 1600 people.

FIRST ORCHESTRA CONCERT:

The Polyhymnia Society was established in St. Louis and performed its first orchestra concert on October 8, 1845. It would be another fifteen years before a full-fledged symphony could be formed.

FIRST SYMPHONY ORCHESTRA:

On June 21, 1860, the Philharmonic Society of St. Louis was established. The St. Louis Philharmonic Orchestra (not to be confused with the St. Louis Symphony) is one of the nation's oldest musical organizations. They played their first concert on October 18, 1860 under the baton of Edouard Sobolowski.

FIRST "STARS & STRIPES":

"Read it and pass it on to a buddy." *The Stars and Stripes*, the famous newspaper for those serving in the military had been printed the night before and was distributed on November 9, 1861 for the first time. This great newspaper for those in uniform was created in Bloomfield, Missouri.

FIRST LARGE THEATER IN KC:

The first large theater in Kansas City, The Coates Opera House, opened on October 6, 1870.

FIRST RADIO STATION:

The oldest radio station west of the Mississippi began audio broadcasting on April 25, 1921. This St. Louis University station claims to be the second oldest station in America. It actually began operating in 1912 but only broadcast in Morse code. WEW stands for We Enlighten the World. KMBZ radio went on the air in Kansas City just less than a year later. It is Missouri's second oldest station and was, for years, owned and operated by rival branches of the Mormon Church.

FIRST BROADCAST NETWORK:

In an early attempt at networking before the days of broadcast networks President Warren G. Harding's speech from the Democrat Convention in St. Louis was sent by telephone lines from KSD radio to other stations in the U.S. This was on June 21, 1923. Then on December 6, 1923, KSD radio in St. Louis joined with four other stations to carry a speech by President Coolidge thus forming something new called a radio "network."

FIRST TELEVISION STATION:

Missouri's first television station, KSDK-TV Went on the air on February 8, 1947. It was the second station west of the Mississippi. Only KTLA-TV in Los Angeles was older. KSD represents the initials of Joseph Pulitzer's grandmother, Kate Star Davis. WDAF-TV went on the air in Kansas City October 16, 1949 and was Missouri's second television station.

FIRST TELEVISED PRESIDENTIAL ADDRESS:

President Harry Truman made history by delivering the first address televised from the White House. The date was October 5, 1947.

FIRST EDUCATIONAL TV STATION:

On May 7, 1953, the FCC approved the start-up of a new TV station by the Educational Television Commission. It would, of course, be KETC in St. Louis.

FIRST NATIONAL TV SHOW FROM MISSOURI:

Beginning on January 22, 1955, the Ozark Jubilee, a national TV show aired from Springfield, MO. It ran for six years and introduced many young stars to the nation. Red Foley was the host.

FIRST TALK RADIO:

Talk Radio began on February 29, 1960. At KMOX in St. Louis, Hall of Fame announcer Jack Buck, interviewed Mayor Tucker, then Eleanor Roosevelt, as they took calls from listeners. The idea worked so well that the station manager ordered employees to get rid of the station's music library. Now stations all across the nation use basically the same format that was pioneered that day.

FIRST CINEMA MULTIPLEX:

In Kansas City, Stanley Durwood opened what is recognized as the first multi-plex cinema on the 12th of July, 1963. His company is now known as AMC Entertainment.

OTHER SIGNIFICANT MISSOURI FIRSTS:

FIRST EUROPEAN TO SEE THE MISSISSIPPI:

De Soto, Missouri is named for Hernando De Soto. On May 8, 1541 DeSoto "discovered" the Mississippi River.

FIRST EUROPEAN TO SEE THE MISSOURI:

On February 2, 1682 René-Robert Cavelier, Sieur de La Salle looked across the Mississippi River and saw what is now Missouri – the first European to do so. He recorded the name "Missouri" for the area meaning it was the place of the big canoes. The explorer, LaSalle, who opened Missouri and the Mississippi Valley for exploration was murdered five years later by mutineers.

FIRST DOCTOR:

Dr. Andre Auguste Conde, the very first medical doctor arrived in Missouri on October 20, 1765 and lived here until his death on November 28, 1776. He was the first physician to live there permanently. Before St. Louis, he served as the post surgeon at Fort Chatres. His home stood where the parking lot for the Old Cathedral is today (under the Arch) Bernard Farr arrived in Missouri in about 1800 becoming the first physician west of the Mississippi.

FIRST POST OFFICE IN SPRINGFIELD:

The Ozarks was just being explored in 1819 and on January 4 of that year Henry Schoolcraft was in the area of Springfield. His glowing description attracted many early settlers to the area. Because of this the area grew rapidly and by January 3, 1834 – The first post office was opened in Springfield. Mail arrived twice each month from Arlington on the Big Piney River.

FIRST SETTLERS IN KANSAS CITY:

It was December 28, 1831, when Rev. Isaac McCoy, a Baptist missionary to the Indians, brought his family to western Missouri. His son, John C. McCoy, would first establish Westport, MO on February 13, 1835. This is considered by many to be the beginning of Kansas City. John C. became wealthy by providing supplies and services for the eventual travelers on the Santa Fe Trail and Oregon Trails.

FIRST UNIVERSITY:

On December 28, 1832, St. Louis University was chartered. This became the first university west of the Mississippi River.

FIRST RAID IN MO-KS BORDER WAR:

On December 20, 1858, John Brown's body wasn't yet "...a-molderin' in the grave." He was busy making his first raid into Missouri to start the border war with Kansas. This was in Vernon County.

FIRST AFRICAN-AMERICAN AMBASSADOR:

James Milton Turner, was born a slave on May 16, 1840. He went on to establish schools for blacks across the state. He was named by Grant as the first African-American to be an Ambassador to another country.

FIRST TYPEWRITER:

Before computers all business correspondence and most assignments in high school and college were typed on type writers. Before keyboarding there was typing. On January 14, 1868 the first and only typewriter in the United States was in use in St. Louis as Charles Weller transcribed court notes.

FIRST PRESIDENT IN KANSAS CITY:

On October 12, 1887, Grover Cleveland became the first President to visit Kansas City.

FIRST ICED TEA:

On June 3, 1904, it was a hot day at the World's Fair. Englishman, Richard Blechynden, couldn't sell his hot tea so he poured it over ice and a line formed. Iced tea was born.

FIRST ICE CREAM CONE:

The International Association of Ice Cream Makers credit Syrian immigrant, Ernest Hamwi, with using his wafer-like pastries to hold a scoop of ice cream on July 29, 1904. (Some insist that it was July 23.) Thus, the ice cream cone was born at World's Fair. He called it a "World's Fair Cornucopia."

FIRST SLEDDING ON ART HILL:

A snowstorm caused cancellation of work for people taking down the World's Fair on January 5, 1905. That day they discovered the fine qualities of the snow-covered hill in front of what is now the Art Museum. It proved to be a great place for toboggans. Today's sledders look for every opportunity to use Art Hill for the same purpose.

Sledding on Art Hill

FIRST PLANNED SUBURBAN COMMUNITY:

The state Legislature approved the incorporation of "Kirkwood Association" on February 8, 1853. It was the first planned suburban community in the United States.

FIRST PONY EXPRESS:

On August 3, 1854 Congress created a Pony Express to operate between Neosho, Missouri and Albuquerque, New Mexico. This was almost six years before the famous route from St. Joseph to Sacramento was started. After less than a year of losing money the route was changed to run from Independence, to Stockton, California via Albuquerque. Why do we never hear about this early southern route Pony Express?

FIRST ST. JOE PONY EXPRESS:

On April 3, 1860 the Pony Express started its first run from St. Joseph. The famous painting, statue, and movie depictions always show the rider speeding away from the starting point at full gallop. Actually he only went a couple of blocks to the riverfront where he had to stop and get on the ferry boat to cross the Missouri River.

FIRST WRITING BY "MARK TWAIN":

He had done some writing under his own name, Samuel Clemens. But on February 2, 1863, Clemens used the name "Mark Twain" for the first time. "Mark Twain" was a good news riverboat term meaning the water is as deep as two marks on a rope. That is two fathoms or about eight feet and deep enough for smooth sailing.

FIRST TIME A MARK TWAIN BOOK WAS BANNED:

On March 17, 1885 – The first library had just banned Mark Twain's new book, "Huckleberry Finn." Twain still felt certain that he could sell at least 25,000 copies. I think he did! Huckleberry Finn is now considered one of the greatest American novels.

FIRST CHALK ERASER:

Professor James T. Dougherty of De Soto patented a chalk eraser for use on blackboards on February 13, 1890.

FIRST AMERICAN CRUISE SHIP:

It was November 9, 1894 when Mrs. Grover Cleveland used a bottle of Missouri wine to christen the *S.S. St. Louis.* It was the very first transatlantic passenger steamship built in the United States.

FIRST SMILING PHOTOGRAPHS:

At a time when photographs of people were supposed to be serious, Jean Tomlinson Frazer encouraged people to smile. Smiling poses came to be known as the "Jean Smile." Say Jean! When her husband, Hal, took a picture of her holding a large catfish she had just caught, Jean was seen to be smiling. Hal touched up the famous photo however, so the fish was smiling too. Jean Tomlinson Frazer was born in Hannibal on March 2, 1894 and began taking the smiling portraits in Hannibal after World War I.

FIRST FAME FOR MISSOURI MULES:

On August 4, 1914, the British Army began using Missouri mules and the mule's reputation was established.

FIRST CONSERVATION COMMISSION:

The very first Missouri Conservation Commission was appointed on July 1, 1937.

FIRST MARRIED TEACHERS:

On March 2, 1944, the Kansas City School Board was having trouble finding teachers during the war so they decided that married women could now be teachers.

FIRST SPRAY CANS:

Inventor, Aaron "Bunny" Lapin was born in St. Louis. During the WWII rationing he invented an oil substitute for whipped cream and called it Reddi-wip. Of course he made it squirt out of a can. He was also the first to market shaving cream in aerosol cans. Since then we have enjoyed spray paint, silly string, and much more.

FIRST RECORDING OF "SWEET BETSY FROM PIKE":

The first recording of "Sweet Betsy from Pike," the famous ballad which tells of Betsy and her uncle, Ike, westward pioneers from Pike County Missouri was released on February 11, 1941.

FIRST POLIO VACCINES:

On April 21, 1955, the first polio vaccines arrived in Missouri. This was the beginning of the end for a terrible childhood disease.

FIRST AMERICAN SPACE SHIP:

On April 2, 1960, McDonnell-Douglas delivered the first of 20 Mercury Space Capsules for NASA. For decades, all of America's space ships would be built in St. Louis.

FIRST BOW ON THE PLANETARIUM:

On Christmas Day, 1966, a group of architecture students from Washington University sneaked into the McDonnell Planetarium and tied a huge red bow around the hyperboloid roof, thus starting the St. Louis Christmas tradition.

Missouri's Last ...

LAST OF THE MISSOURI TRIBE:

The sad remains of the Missouri Tribe appeared at St. Louis on October 10, 1764. The 400 demanded that they be allowed to live in the town. They demanded provisions and then stole them. Most of the colonists fled across the Mississippi until Pierre Laclede talked the Indians into leaving. That was the last time they were seen in this territory. There were eventually just a few remaining and they joined with their cousins, the Oto, and moved to a reservation in the Indian Territory. (Oklahoma) The last of the Missouris died on that reservation in 1907.

THE LAST SHAWNEE IN MISSOURI:

Of course we still have individual Shawnee and Shawnee families in the state but on November 7, 1825, the Shawnee Nation gave up all lands within Missouri in exchange for land in other territories.

LAST DAY AT THE FIRST CAPITAL:

January 21, 1826 was the last day to meet in the first capital building in St. Charles.

LAST WHIPPING POSTS AND PILLORIES:

The State Legislature outlawed the use of whipping posts and the pillory as punishment for crimes on December 30, 1826. The whipping post held a person in place while being lashed with a leather bull whip. The pillory held a person's head and wrists while they endured humiliation or physical pain.

LAST OF THE INDIAN LANDS IN MISSOURI:

It was October 24, 1832, when the last Indian lands in Missouri were given up. The Kickapoo Nation surrendered over 2 million acres in Missouri for about one third that much in Kansas. They also got $18,000. They are still remembered and honored in Southwest Missouri with street names, high schools, and more.

LAST OF THE BLACKSNAKE HILLS TRADING POST:

Actually this important post didn't come to an end – it just underwent a name change. On November 20, 1843 the folks living at the Blacksnake Hills Trading Post changed their town's name to St. Joseph, Missouri.

THE LAST DEBTORS PRISON:

The practice of imprisoning debtors was outlawed on January 17, 1843.

THE LAST PONY EXPRESS RUN:

With all telegraph lines in place the Pony Express was no longer needed. On November 20, 1861, the riders made their last run and closed one of the most exciting chapters in American History.

THE LAST SLAVE AUCTION:

On New Year's Day, 1861, the last slave auction was held in St. Louis. 2000 people showed up to jeer and interrupt the proceedings. Finally the auctioneer gave up and the event was ended.

THE LAST OF BLOODY BILL:

Guerrilla fighter, William Anderson (Bloody Bill) was reported killed in Ray County on October 26, 1864. His head was put on a pole and his body dragged through the streets of Richmond, MO. (It was realized later that it might not have been him.)

LAST OF MOUND CITY'S MOUNDS:

St. Louis was known as "Mound City" for many years. This was due to the Indian mounds in the area. The largest, Big Mound, was destroyed beginning on November 8, 1868. Along with it, untold amounts of Mississippian cultural artifacts were also destroyed.

THE LAST LARGE CATTLE DRIVES IN ST. LOUIS:

On June 22, 1873 – St. Louis citizens were demanding that cattle no longer be allowed in the streets. A Texas steer had just charged down Lucas street killing an elderly woman. So on July 11, 1873, the city banned cattle herds in the streets except between the hours of 10:00 PM and 6:00 AM and they must be brought through in herds of 25 or fewer.

THE LAST COWS LEGALLY IN ST. LOUIS:

People were still upset about cows in St. Louis. Horses were necessary but not cows. On June 12, 1877, the court in St. Louis was debating the issue of people keeping livestock on their property. In a protest, a lady known only as Mrs. Muldoon led a group of 150 angry people to a city pen and released 150 stray cows. Soon even milk cows were banned but many people secretly continued to keep one in their own back yards.

LAST DAY OF THE WORLD'S FAIR:

On December 1, 1904 David Francis said, "Farewell to all thy splendor." and threw a switch closing the wonderful World's Fair.

LAST STAGE COACHES IN MISSOURI:

Though the principal job of stage coaches was carrying mail, many people depended on them for transportation between the various towns and even between various communities in urban areas. While railroads connected many large communities, folks would often have to get of the railroad coach and onto a stage coach to complete their journey. This was the case until 1916 when the last stage coach in Missouri completed its final run and was replaced by a motor bus.

THE LAST DAY TO GET A (LEGAL) DRINK:

June 15, 1919 was the last day to legally buy anything alcoholic in the nation. On the 16th, the prohibition amendment was ratified. Then came stills in the hills.

LAST GOTHIC BUILDING:

The cornerstone was laid for the Memorial Union Tower at the University of Missouri on November 29, 1922. It is the last gothic structure to be erected in the United States.

Memorial Union Tower
at Mizzou

LAST DAY FOR THE PLANTERS HOTEL:

On New Year's Eve, 1922, the history-laden Planters Hotel in St. Louis closed its doors. In addition to all the dignitaries who frequented the place, the famous bartender invented one drink he called Planter's Punch and then another he named for himself, Tom Collins.

THE LAST FIRE HORSES:

The last fire horses known to this writer were retired from the St. Louis Fire Department on February 1, 1927. The final 32 had been pulling pumper wagons but now everything would be motorized.

LAST FLIGHT FOR THE SPIRIT OF ST. LOUIS:

On April 30, 1928, *The Spirit of St. Louis* flew its last flight, departing from Lambert Field and arriving in Washington, D.C., where it was subsequently donated to the Smithsonian Institution.

THE LAST HANGING:

On New Year's Eve, 1930, at the old Jail and Hanging Barn in Boonville, Lawrence Mabry climbed the 13 steps to the loft and was hanged for a killing in Pettis County. This was the last public hanging in Missouri. The old Cooper County Jail and Hanging Barn was in continuous use from 1848 until 1978. It had also been used as a "bull pen" to hold slaves prior to auction.

LAST OF THE WORST(?) RAILROAD:

July 10, 1934, was the last day of operation for what some people considered the worst railroad in the state. "The Leaky Roof Railroad" between Springfield and Kansas City ceased operations on that day.

LAST LOG LIBRARY:

The grand opening of the beautiful little cypress log library at Puxico was on July 15, 1939. This was the last library to be constructed of logs in the state and possibly in the nation.

The Puxico Library

THE LAST LYNCHING:

A man in Sikeston seems to have broken into a home and stabbed a lady. Upon being arrested he is said to have stabbed a Marshall. I cannot describe here the horrific details of his January 25, 1942 lynching, but it was the last in Missouri.

THE LAST BATTLESHIP:

The last and largest battleship ever built, The U.S.S. Missouri was launched on January 29, 1944. The historic ship on which World War II ended was decommissioned on March 31, 1992 in preparation for becoming a museum at Pearl Harbor. In addition to this "Mighty Mo," there have been four other ships-of-the-line named for the Show-Me State. The current USS Missouri is a nuclear attack submarine commissioned on July 31, 2010.

THE LAST GREAT STEAMBOAT:

The Golden Eagle, last of the Eagle Packet steamboats was bound for Nashville from St. Louis when it sank near Tower Rock and Altenburg on May 18, 1947. Of course there are still many riverboats but they are powered by diesel engines.

THE LAST WOODEN-HULLED PASSENGER BOAT:

The last wooden-hulled passenger boat on the Mississippi departed St. Louis on its final voyage January 19, 1953. The *St. Paul*, also known as *The Excursion Queen*, was 70 years old.

LAST GAME FOR "THE BROWNIES":

Way back on December 3, 1901, the Milwaukee team announced their move to St. Louis to become the Browns. St. Louis would then be known as "First in beer, first in shoes, and last in the American League." They had some wonderful and colorful years, but the Cardinals proved to be so popular that the Browns couldn't draw enough fans. They also made some bad decisions which resulted in explosions and fires at the park. So on September 29, 1953, they called it quits. The St. Louis Browns were so "broke" that they ran out of baseballs during their last game! Sadly, the Brownies left town to become the Baltimore Orioles.

THE LAST OF THE GREAT TRAINS:

Missouri Pacific's last steam engines pulled into the scrap yard on April 7, 1957. All were replaced by diesels.

The last KATY passenger train made its final run across Missouri on May Day, 1958. Prior to this there were 115 trains per day using Union Station in St. Louis. Other passenger lines soon followed suit as travelers moved toward interstate highways and aviation.

THE LAST OF THE GREAT TRAINS: (Continued)

The *Wabash Cannonball* and the *Midnight Special* made nostalgia runs to Union Station in St. Louis on April 30, 1971. This was the last day for private rail service in the state. The next day Amtrak went into operation and the government cut service back to four trains a day.

THE LAST SERVICE CARS:

At one time more than 500 service cars cruised around St. Louis acting as small busses. This angered the cab drivers and the bus company. So, on November 30, 1965 the last of the oversized autos made the final run around town.

THE LAST OF THE ST. LOUIS CHINATOWN:

On August 20, 1966, the final buildings in St. Louis' "Chinatown" came down on this date to make room for a stadium parking garage. This was part of a project to give us Busch Stadium #2 but we lost a colorful neighborhood with great restaurants.

LAST GAME FOR THE KANSAS CITY A's:

The Kansas City Athletics (Now the Oakland A's) played their last game on October 1, 1967.

THE LAST OF ROUTE 66:

The last "Route 66" shields were removed from the final 14-mile stretch between Scotland, Missouri and the Kansas line on July 24, 1985. With that, the Mother Road was no more.

THE LAST GUBERBURGERS:

No more GuberBurgers! The Wheel In Drive In had been serving burgers at the intersection of Highways 50 and 65 in Sedalia since 1947. Their claim to fame was the GuberBurger which was a hamburger covered with melted peanut butter, lettuce, and mayonnaise. Due to road widening, the place closed on September 3, 2007.

LAST DAY FOR THE RIVERBOAT McDONALDS:

On November 7, 2000, the Riverboat McDonald's below the Gateway Arch closed its doors. This writer spent many a pleasant morning with coffee and an Egg McMuffin watching the city come alive from the top deck.

Missouri's Greatest . . . (Heros)

On May 4, 1819, nineteen-year-old **Henry Shaw** arrived in Missouri. He stepped off the steamboat *Maid of Orleans,* made a fortune, then retired to look for ways to use his money helping people. He started the Missouri Botanical Gardens at his home, then Shaw Park, schools, hospitals, and he endowed universities.

On June 26, 1846, **Colonel Alexander Doniphan** left with a battalion of Missouri troops on this day for an expedition into Mexico. This battalion captured Chihuahua and Saltillo even though they were outnumbered and outgunned. Then they proceeded to capture Monterrey. They came home as national heroes.

Colonel Alexander Doniphan and **Colonel Sterling Price** commanding the First and Second Missouri Volunteers, defeated a superior force of Mexican troops at the Battle of Sacramento Pass on February 28, 1847. It turned the course of the war toward an American victory. They were under the command of **General Stephen Kearney.**

Joseph Conway

December 14, 1763 is the birthday of Joseph Conway for whom Conway Road in St. Louis County is named. He was possibly the toughest man in our history. This Indian fighter was said by Ripley's to have been tomahawked three times, shot three times, and left for dead three times.

Annie Baxter

Annie White Baxter was born on March 2, 1864. Ms. Baxter was elected to the position of Jasper County Clerk. An amazing accomplishment since her election was a full thirty years before women were even allowed to vote.

Cathay Williams

Born a slave in Independence, MO, Cathay Williams enlisted in the U.S. Army at Jefferson Barracks in St. Louis on November 15, 1866. She had run away to the army during the Civil War and served the army as a collateral laborer. She enlisted as a man calling herself William Cathay and served in the famous Buffalo Soldiers Regiment. Only two other women were ever known to have done this. They were Cathay's cousin and a good friend. They all served together as Buffalo Soldiers.

President and General Hiram Ulysses Grant (aka Ulysses S. Grant)

Life was tough for Grant and his wife Julia Dent. On their "Hardscrabble Farm" in St. Louis County, the future looked bleak. Grant had been good as a military officer while stationed at Jefferson Barracks but the rest of his life saw little success. Then came the War Between the States and he was called back into the military. Of course we know that he went on to command the Union's forces and to become President of the U.S.

John Berry Meachum

It was not terribly unusual for a black man to own slaves but John Berry Meachum was a hero for doing so. He became rich making barrels, salvaging sunken steamboats, and operating his own steamboat line. With his money he purchased many slaves with the intent of setting them free as soon as they met two qualifications. They must learn a job skill to support themselves and their family, and they must get a rudimentary education to prevent being cheated out of what they had earned.

Meachum also started "The Freedom School" for St. Louis blacks and his house was a stop on the underground railway.

The **Houn' Dawgs** were formed on February 21, 1891. The second Missouri Division, U.S. Army was formed on this date. Their famous Taney County song, *Houn'Dawg*, told of a loyal and protective hound. The song continued with the group and by World War I they were all known as The Houn'Dawgs. At this writing, the 203rd Missouri National Guard proudly carries that name into battle in Afghanistan.

"Jim seen his duty there an' then,

He lit into them gentlemen;

He shore mussed up the courthouse square

With rags an' meat an' hide an' hair."

Insignia for the Houn'Dawgs

Neosho-born inventor, pilot, and daredevil, **Hugh Armstrong Robinson** was the third person (after the two Wright brothers) to fly an airplane. In fact, his flying teachers were Orville and Wilbur Wright. He was the first person to make an air-sea rescue and he survived 15 crashes. In 1911 he was a leader of early flight operations centered around Monett, Neosho, Carthage, and Joplin.

On April 11, 1877, fireman **Phelim O'Toole** became a legend. The Southern Hotel was on fire and about a dozen people were trapped beyond the reach of ladders. O'Toole swung on a rope to reach tied-together bedsheets then climbed up the sheets and brought all the people to safety. St. Louis citizens awarded O'Toole a check for $500.00 which he immediately donated to an orphan's fund. Several months later the Old Courthouse was on fire and seemed doomed. O'Toole climbed up onto its dome and chopped his way through. Then, hose in hand, he hung down inside the dome and fought the fire from the most advantageous angle. On July 6, 1880, O'Toole was putting out a routine small fire when the extinguisher in his hands blew up and killed him. Over 20,000 people lined the route of his funeral procession.

Uriel Sebree, from Fayette, Missouri served as Commander-in-Chief of the Pacific Fleet, Arctic Explorer, Governor of American Samoa.

In Houston, Missouri on November 3, 1912, wind scattered sparks from the Lone Star Mill, which furnished electricity for the town, and the sparks caught the mill's roof on fire. **Albert Raper**, a young man, climbed to the high steep roof and having no water, "tore the blazing shingles off and soon conquered the blaze." The citizens of Houston gave him a gold watch for his bravery.

General of the Armies, John J. (Black Jack) Pershing was born in Laclede, Missouri September 13, 1860. He was leader of all allied forces during World War I.

On July 31, 1951, Kirksville papers were carrying the story of the death of local hero, **James Reiger.** After graduating from KHS, he graduated from NEMSU (now Truman State) and the University of Missouri in Columbia. In World War I he became "the Hero of the Argonne" and was awarded the Distinguished Service Cross, France's *Croix de Guerre*, and more.

On Pearl Harbor Day, December 7, 1941, **George A. Whiteman** from Sedalia was shot down as his plane took off from Hawaii. He became the first pilot killed in World War II. Whiteman Air Force Base near Sedalia is named in his honor.

Missourian, **James H. Howard** got separated from his fighter group and, all alone, attacked a German flight of thirty planes on January 11, 1944. He shot down six. He had earlier recorded six kills while serving with the "Flying Tigers" in Asia. He was therefore the first ace in both of those theaters of operation. Howard was given the Congressional Medal of Honor.

James H. Howard

Black aviator, **Wendell Pruitt**, was honored in his home town of St. Louis on December 12, 1944. He won the Distinguished Flying Cross for shooting down three German planes, destroying 70 on the ground and helping to sink a German destroyer. He was killed while training other black pilots for the "Tuskegee Airmen."

Lt. Col. John England was born on January 15, 1923 in Caruthersville. He participated in 108 combat missions during World War II, Destroyed 19 German aircraft. On one mission he downed four enemy planes. He died by sacrificing himself and his damaged plane to avoid harming friendly forces.

Lt. Col. John B. England

General Omar Bradley was given a huge ticker tape parade on June 11, 1945. Known as "The Soldier's General" he was Commander of the 12th Army during World War II. Eventually he reached the rank of five star General and Chairman of the Joint Chiefs of Staff.

General Jimmy Doolittle

James Doolittle was born on December 14, 1896. On January 15, 1930, Lieutenant James Doolittle arrived in St. Louis to serve as Director of Aviation Activities for Shell Oil Company. On September 2, 1931, he set a new transcontinental flight record (Newark to Burbank in just over 11 hours) and claimed the Bendix Trophy with a $10,000 prize.

On August 29, 1932 Ferguson, Missouri resident, James Hailslip, set a new speed record for transcontinental flight breaking the old record by St. Louis native, Jimmy Doolittle. But Doolittle wasn't finished making important flights. On April 18, 1942 Doolittle was chosen to lead the first bombing raid on Tokyo in World War II. Flying another plane with Doolittle that day was **Major Thomas "Tom" Griffin** from Florissant, Missouri.

In honor of the brave leader of the "Thirty Seconds Over Tokyo," Centerville (west of Rolla on Route 66) was re-named for the leader of the raid, Jimmy Doolittle on October 11, 1946. General Doolittle himself was there for the ceremony.

It was February 23, 1945 when **Lieutenant Harold George Schrier** led a group of US Marines up Mount Suribachi and planted a flag at her top signaling the great victory at Iwo Jima. He and his companions are depicted in the Iwo Jima monument in the nation's capital. Schrier was born at Corder, MO and want to school at Lexington, MO.

Iwo Jima Memorial

May 1, 1999 was the opening day for **Jim the Wonder Dog** Park in Marshall, MO. It commemorates the most amazing animal in American history. And, yes, he was truly a hero to the Americans of his day so he is included here. Read more about him and you will be amazed.

Missouri's Oldest...

OLDEST TOWN:

On January 3, 1735, the village of Ste. Genevieve was founded by French trappers and miners. French settlers had been living in the area for three years prior to that. (Residents of Old Mines, Missouri lay claim to this title also.)

OLDEST PROTESTANT CEMETERY NORTH OF MISSOURI RIVER:

This cemetery was established on March 18, 1813 with the burial of Rebecca Bryan Boone. She and her husband Daniel, were living with their adopted son, David Bryan, at the time. The family buried her next to an apple orchard that she loved and Daniel was buried with her seven years later. This is near the village of pioneer village of Charette (near present day Marthasville, Missouri).

OLDEST INDEPENDENCE DAY PARADE:

Marshfield, MO had an Independence Day celebration and parade in 1880. Now that parade stands as the oldest continuous 4th of July celebration in America. The amazing and wonderful part of this story is that this first parade was staged just a few weeks after the town was destroyed by a terrible F-4 tornado. (Read about the April 18, 1880 event in the "Disasters" section of this book.) The parade was a show of their pioneer determination.

OLDEST BRASS BAND:

The El Dorado Springs Municipal Band played its first concert on May Day, 1896. It has played several concerts a week through all the warm weather months in every year since. It seems to be the oldest community band in the nation. The Washington Brass Band (Washington, MO) is approximately the same age but the exact beginning has not been pinpointed.

OLDEST FARMERS MARKETS:

Way back on February 10, 1843, Mrs. Jilia Soulard gave the city of St. Louis a gift of land on the south side. The gift stipulated that it must be used as a public market. Soulard Market has been a landmark for over 170 years now. On August 8, 1888 the little Ozarks community of Ozark, MO opened a Farmers Market and it has been providing fresh produce and more ever since.

OLDEST JEWISH TEMPLE:

The cornerstone was laid on April 16, 1855 for the B'Nai El Temple which is home for the oldest Reform Jewish congregation west of the Mississippi.

OLDEST FAIR:

The Moniteau County Agricultural and Mechanical Society had a fair on August 8, 1859. It stands now as the oldest continuously held fair. (Now called the Moniteau County Fair)

OLDEST PEOPLE:

This is a category that keeps changing as the years go by and as we all live a little longer than the generation before us. Having said that, here are a few of the very oldest Missourians.

* Miriam Bannister lived to be 111 years and 21 days old. She died in 1986.

* Emma Wilson reached the age of 113 years and 54 days before her death in 1983.

* Henry Dorman of Liberal, MO died in March of 1914 and was thought to be 115 years old at that time. He was, until that time, America's oldest living veteran of the Civil War. This was because he didn't enlist until he was 64. He was born eleven months prior to the death of George Washington so that meant that he was the only person to live during the lives of every single American President! He was also alive in the 18th, 19th, and 20th Centuries.

* Augusta Holtz saw an amazing 115 years and 79 days living from 8-3-71 to 10-21-1986. She was the world's oldest verified person. She was also the very first person in the history of the world to reach 115 years. Ms. Holtz was born in Eastern Prussia and died in Florissant, Missouri.

OLDEST CHURCH:

Missouri's only saint, Rose Philippine Duchesne of St. Charles, Florissant, and St. Louis, assisted in laying the cornerstone of St. Ferdinand's in Florissant on February 19, 1821. It is the oldest Catholic church building between the Mississippi and the Rockies.

OLDEST NEWSPAPER:

The Missouri Whig and General Advertiser, a newspaper in Palmyra, was first printed on August 3, 1839. The newspaper still operates in Palmyra (now known as the *Palmyra Spectator*) and is the oldest Missouri newspaper in continuous operation.

OLDEST FOOTBALL STADIUM:

The stadium at Northwest Missouri State University was opened in 1917 and is therefore the oldest stadium in America's Division II schools.

OLDEST COMMUNITY PICNIC:

Sheldon, Missouri had its very first Old Settlers Picnic on August 27, 1904. It continues today as it has for over a century.

Missouri's Best . . . (Sports)

There is a special category here for **Robert Calvin (Cal) Hubbard** was born in Keytesville, MO. Born on Halloween day in 1900, he spent his life in sports and is enshrined in the Baseball Hall of Fame, the Football Hall of Fame, and the College Football Hall of Fame.

BASEBALL & SOFTBALL RECORDS:

To test the market for professional baseball, a team of professional players played an amateur all-star team in St. Louis on March 27, 1875. The All Stars won 15 to 0. One thousand people attended the game. The next year the city got a pro team which later became known as the Cardinals.

St. Louis and seven other baseball teams organized the **National League** on February 2, 1876.

On July 15, 1876, **George "Grins" Bradley** threw the first no-hit, no run game in major league history. Pitching for the St. Louis Brown Stockings that year, he completed 63 of the team's 64 games. He won 45 of them and ended the season with a 1.23 e.r.a. His 16 shutouts that year set a record that has never been broken. (Of course Brown Stockings was an early name for the Cardinals.)

On April 30 , 1887, the **Browns** set a Missouri professional baseball scoring record when they beat Cleveland 28-11.

Pitching great, **John Donaldson** was born in Glasgow, MO on February 29, 1892. A phenomenal baseball pitcher playing long before black men were allowed in the major leagues, he was spotted by Tug McGraw of the N.Y. Giants and offered $50,000 if he would go to Cuba and play for a year. Then McGraw could draft him for the Giants as a Cuban. Donaldson turned down the offer because he refused to renounce his family or his race.

Cy Young pitched his first game for St. Louis on April 15, 1899. Of course the Cy Young award for each season's outstanding pitcher is named for him.

On August 30, 1902, Joplin's first professional baseball team, the **Colts**, played their home opener on this day. Other teams in their Missouri Valley League included some from Arkansas, Kansas, and Oklahoma as well as Springfield, Rolla, Nevada, Sedalia, and Jefferson City. This writer appreciates people who don't take themselves too seriously and thinks he would enjoy a league which chooses names for itself like the Nevada **Lunatics**, the Sedalia **Gold Bugs**, the Jefferson City **Convicts**, and the Iola **Gasbags**.

May 17, 1903, was the birthday of St. Louis resident, **James Thomas "Cool Papa" Bell**, a Baseball Hall of Famer who played with St. Louis Stars, Kansas City Stars, and Kansas City Monarchs – all in the Negro Leagues. He is considered the fastest man who ever played the game.

Legendary sports broadcaster, Harry Christopher Carabina (**Harry Caray**) was born in St. Louis on March 1, 1914. He did the broadcasts for Mizzou football, St. Louis Hawks basketball, St. Louis Cardinals, and the St. Louis Browns as well as three other major league baseball teams.

In 1887 **George H. Rawlings** opened a popular sporting goods store in St. Louis. He sold the gloves that all baseball players used in those days. They were just regular gloves but a little larger and with a little padding. In 1919 a Cardinals pitcher asked George Rawlings' firm to make a glove with a web between the thumb and the forefinger. This set the pattern for all future baseball gloves and started the Rawlings Sporting Goods Company with several manufacturing locations in Missouri.

At Cycle Park in Joplin the famous **Bloomer Girls** professional baseball team was playing a group of local all stars on July 3, 1898. They often came to Joplin, Springfield, Columbia, Jefferson City and other places and they usually won. They always played men's teams and the men from Joplin were among the few teams that could often beat the ladies.

The Bloomer Girls were a very successful franchise and they won most of their games. One reason for this was that they had "ringers" on the team. Two or three men would dress as women and add punch to the lineup. One of these men was a young guy getting his start in pro ball. **Rogers Hornsby** would go from the barnstorming Bloomer Girls to the St. Louis Cardinals and the Hall of Fame.

"Casey" Stengel, named for his home town of K.C., stunned jeering baseball fans on June 6, 1918 by bowing to them and ceremoniously tipping his cap. From under the hat a bird flew out. Casey may have been the first player to "give the fans the bird."

On February 14, 1920 in Kansas City, **Rube Foster** organized the Negro National League. Both St. Louis and Kansas City were among the original franchises. This league brought opportunities for many great ball players and good quality enjoyment for the fans.

February 2, 1923 is the birthday of Hall of Famer, **Red Schoendienst** who as player, coach, and manager spent 45 years in a Cardinals uniform!

THE HALL OF FAME STREET

Narrow little Elizabeth Street (St. Louis) with all the tiny houses was named "Hall of Fame Place" in honor of its former residents, **Yogi Berra**, **Jack Buck**, and **Joe Garagiola.**

Hall of Fame Cardinal broadcaster, Jack Buck, lived on that street early in his career and in the mid-1920s Yogi Berra and Joe Garagiola were born there. Of course Jack Buck gained fame as the Cardinals Broadcaster and Joe was a catcher for the Cardinals. Yogi was offered the job before Joe but the Cardinals wouldn't give him the $500 signing bonus that the Yankees offered. Offended by that $500, Yogi left for New York.

Joe Garagiola reported that every other player in the pros was the best on his high school team, and the best in his home town, and the best on his college team. Joe, on the other hand, wasn't even the best player on his block. When they chose teams, Yogi was always picked first.

A young pitcher, **Jerome Dean**, broke in with the minor league St. Joseph Saints on April 20, 1930. Of course the world came to know him as Dizzy Dean. While in the army, Jerome Dean was told to do K.P. duty and, at 5:30 AM, a sergeant walked in on him "pitching" potatoes at a trash can lid. The sergeant called him a "dizzy son-of-a-b***h" and the name stuck.

April 30, 1931 was the opening day for the Joplin Miners minor league baseball team. A large crowd was on hand to see **Vada Corbus**, a pioneering woman catcher, start the game on this formerly all-male team. However, a story in the New York Times had alerted league officials who banned her from playing. (This was also the first professional team for a young Mickey Mantle.)

Vada Corbus

in her 1931

Joplin Miners Uniform

On March 22, 1934, a woman pitched for the Cardinals. **Babe Didrickson** was the starter in an exhibition game against the Red Sox. She gave up four hits and three runs and was knocked out in the first inning.

The Cardinals signed a young pitcher on June 5, 1937. The man hurt his arm so the team moved the pitcher, **Stanley Musial**, to the outfield. He did OK there and finished a long career with a career batting average of .331! On February 15, 2011 "Baseball's perfect warrior, baseball's perfect knight," hall of famer, "Stan the Man" Musial was awarded the Presidential Medal of Freedom.

One-armed outfielder, **Pete Gray**, played his first game for the Browns on April 18, 1945. He was a good man in the field and batted .218 in his one season with the team.

On August 28, 1945 K.C. Monarchs star, **Jackie Robinson**, signed to play in the Major Leagues. For many black players this would allow new opportunities but it was the beginning of the end for the Negro League.

The English Teachers Association of Missouri filed a complaint with the F.C.C. on July 11, 1946. They were concerned about **Dizzy Dean**'s influence on the kids. To Dizzy, the past tense of slide was "slud." In his "plain ol' ordinary pinto bean English" he described players who "throwed" balls and walked to the plate "confidentially." They looked "hitterish" and "swang" at pitches. Sometimes they returned to their "respectable" bases. He battled them but the teachers won and he tried harder to use proper grammar.

On February 9, 1951, **Satchel Paige** was signed to pitch for the St. Louis Browns at age 46. People teased him about being so old so, between innings Paige lounged in a rocking chair near the dugout. You will remember that Paige had been a huge star for the Kansas City Monarchs for many years prior to this. He was such a great player that he was still playing professional baseball at age 59.

Satchel Paige was a wonderful pitcher and also a showman. He was said to have used a gum wrapper for home plate when he warmed up. It is claimed that, in crucial situations, he would turn and tell his outfielders to sit down on the grass and he would just strike the next batters out. On February 10, 1971 the great pitcher was inducted into Baseball's Hall of Fame. He died on June 8, 1982.

On May 2, 1954, **Stan Musial** hit five home runs in one day (It was a double header.) He went 6 for 8 that day with 21 total bases. In attendance on that exact day was eight year-old Nate Colbert who would become the only other player to hit five home runs in a double header. On May 13, 1958, Stan the Man got his 3000th hit on this day. Better yet, it was against the Cubs.

Kansas City and St. Louis star, **Al Hrabosky**, (the Mad Hungarian) turned his back on a batter for the first time on June 11, 1974.

The Cardinals played the longest game in their history and the second-longest in MLB history on September 11, 1974. After trailing the Mets 3-1 in the ninth, the Cards came back to tie and then play an additional 15 innings lasting for over seven hours. Finally, at 3:13 A.M., Calloway County's **Bake McBride** scored the winning run.

On September 23, 1979 **Lou Brock** stole his 938th base after hitting his 3,000[th] hit .

Royals Hall of Famer, **George Brett**, played 21 years for Kansas City and got more hits than any other third baseman in history. On July 24, 1983, the famous Pine Tar Incident happened with Brett disputing a strange call by the umpire crew. The "Ump." claimed that the pine tar on Brett's bat was too close to his hands and took away a home run the third baseman had just hit.

On September 8, 1998, **Mark McGuire** hit his 62nd home run breaking the record formerly held by Royals-Yankees-Cardinals great, **Roger Maris**.

The girls' softball team at **Salisbury High School** completed a 38-game winning streak on September 6, 2003.

FOOTBALL RECORDS:

Missouri School of Mines 1914 Football Team

The 1914 football team at the **Missouri School of Mines** in Rolla (Missouri S&T University) was the national champion for college football. They are sometimes cited as the best college football team of all times. Their record was 9-0 and they scored 567 points that year and allowed opponents only six points total for the year!

On October 30, 1900, the entire **University of Missouri** football team resigned. They were upset because the university was requiring that players be full-time students with good grades.

On Nov. 15, 1915, **Sikeston High School** toppled Kennett in football, 147-0.

On October 4, 1919, the **Sikeston H.S.** football team defeated Caruthersville by a score of 148-0. What do they feed those boys at Sikeston?

Rams running back and art student, **Fred Gehrke**, painted rams horns on the side of his brown leather helmet on September 2, 1948. The team paid him $1.00 for each additional helmet and soon the Rams and every NFL team had painted helmets.

A University of Kansas football team on probation played a running back who was ineligible as they beat Number 1, Missouri on November 19, 1960. Then Kansas was caught and had to forfeit the game letting the **University of Missouri** go on to beat Navy in the Orange bowl and remain Number 1 in the nation. Kansans have a different take on the story. They always do.

The football team at **Valle High School** in Ste. Genevieve beat St. Vincent (Perryville) 39-0 on September 10, 1966. That was the beginning of the season for what is called America's greatest high school team ever. Valle averaged 53.5 points per game that year while allowing opponents not one single point for the entire season!

Since the inception of the state football championship tournament, the **Jefferson City Jays** have won 10 state championships, more than any other school in Missouri. In 2004, JCHS became the first public high school to win 600 games. During the 1960s, the team had the highest winning percentage in the nation for that period in time: 94.8%.

Losing a game to their rivals, **Columbia Hickman,** in 1966 ended their longest winning streak. The Jays had won 71 games in a row which was America's longest winning streak.

Marceline's High School football team set a record by winning a low-scoring game against Brookfield on August 31, 1990. The final score was 2-0. This was actually a good win when seen in perspective. You see, in 1913 Marceline's football Team lost to Carrollton by a score of 148-0. To be fair, this 1913 contest was Marceline's first game and the boys on the team had never seen an actual football.

On January 30, 2000, the **St. Louis Rams** were in the Super Bowl to play the Tennessee Titans in what some writers described as the most exciting Super Bowl ever. Yes, the Rams won.

BASKETBALL RECORDS:

Back on April 5, 1928, **Oregon, Missouri's High School** basketball team won again and qualified for the quarterfinals in the National Interscholastic Basketball Tournament. They had earlier won the State Championship in Missouri. At this time the schools were not grouped by size so little Oregon knocked off all of the big schools from the big cities to become State Champs. **Wilbur "Sparky" Stalcup** was their star.

The All American Redheads, a women's professional basketball team sailed to represent America in the Philippine Islands on April 17, 1940. Started by **C. M. Olson** in Cassville, their fame and popularity grew as they played, and almost always beat, men's teams. Their international fame came after a string of 96 wins in 96 days! They were inducted into the Basketball Hall of Fame in 2012.

A Missouri favorite, **Bill Bradley**, was in the Basketball Hall of Fame, a Rhodes Scholar, and U.S. Senator. He was born on July 28, 1943 in Crystal City, MO and grew up there.

On January 18, 2004, **Tyler Hansbrough** from Poplar Bluff High School was playing in the Tournament of Champions at Missouri State University when he had a perfect shooting game. The junior went 12-for-12 from the field (including 2-for-2 from beyond the arc) and 9-for-9 from the free throw line in the contest against Kickapoo (Springfield). He finished with 35 points, 13 rebounds and 5 assists. Yes, this is the same Tyler Hansbrough you know from the NBA.

The NAIA was formed in Kansas City on March 10, 1940. It has actually been conducting a national basketball tournament there since 1937. That year, 1940, the national Division 1 champion basketball team was little **Tarkio College** from Tarkio, MO. Other not-so-surprising national champs included **Central Missouri State** (1937 & 1938), **Southeast Missouri State** (beating runner-up **Northeast Missouri State** in 1943), **Southwest Missouri State** (1952 & 1953), and **Drury** (1979).

It was "a tale of two kitties" on February 10, 2006. The **Marquand Tigers** ran into some bad luck when they played the **Patton Panthers** on this day. The boys' basketball team from Patton set a national record for the number of three-pointers (36) in a single high school basketball game. That's 108 points without even counting the two-pointers and free throws!

On April 7, 2013, **Drury University** in Springfield, claimed the National Championship on this day in Division II Basketball.

The longest marathon game of basketball (and possibly highest scoring) was 112 hours and 13 seconds. This World Record was set at the Missouri Athletic Club in Saint Louis, Missouri, from March 21-25, 2012. **A team from Joplin** defeated another **team from St. Louis** by a score of 11,806 - 11,620. Proceeds from the game went to disaster relief after the Joplin tornado.

OLYMPICS RECORDS:

On February 11, 1903, the International Olympic Committee announced that the 1904 games were being taken from Chicago and would be contested in St. Louis instead. Do you think the folks in Chicago were a little upset? At any rate, on July 1, 1904 The Olympic Games began in St. Louis and continued for several weeks.

On August 17 **George Eyser** had a good day at the Olympic Games. He won gold in the parallel bars and rope climb and tied for gold in the vault. He won silver on the pommel horse and the all-around. He took the bronze medal on the horizontal bars. Pretty good for a guy with one wooden leg!

Then on August 29, the Track and Field events began. A new event, the decathlon, was won by an Irishman, **Tom Kiely**. **George Poage** became the first black man ever to compete in the Olympics and he stayed in St. Louis to coach and teach at Sumner High School.

The Olympics had been over but some results were still in question on September 9. The Milwaukee team was found to be professionals so they had to relinquish their gold medal for tug-of-war. They were tug-of-war professionals?!

The star of the 1936 Olympics in Berlin was the fastest woman in the world, **Helen Stephens** from Fulton, MO. Known internationally as "The Fulton Flash." After she won so many gold medals, Adolph Hitler wanted to meet her. She said he tried to hug her but, "All he got from me was a good old Missouri handshake."

OTHER SPORTS RECORDS:

January 2, 1871 was the birthday of **"Tex" Rickard** who was known as the greatest prize fight promoter of all time. He was born in Clay County, on a farm next to Jesse James' home.

Talk about a hunting trip! On January 4, 1874 the *Cassville Democrat* reported that a man had just come back from hunting with 100 mink skins, 550 coon skins, and three deer skins.

St. Louis saloon-keeper and boxer, **Tom Allen**, won the bare-knuckle boxing championship of the world in London on November 16, 1877.

December 12, 1912 was the birthday of St. Louis prizefighter, **Henry Armstrong** who scored 152 victories and held championship titles in three weight divisions at the same time. He won his first world title on October 29, 1937. He won that one in the Featherweight Division.

St. Louis boxer, **Archie Moore** was born on December 13, 1916. He scored at least 131 knockouts in 27 years and held the heavyweight title from 1952 to 1961. As a prize fighter he won 228 fights (140 of them by knockouts including TKOs). After retirement he worked as an instructor for Cassius Clay, a motivational speaker, and he started an organization to help underprivileged boys.

On June 8, 1923, the national dance marathon was narrowing down at the St. Louis Coliseum. 18-year-old **Hilda Johnson** dropped out after 147 hours. She got a world's record and $700. Three men were still dancing.

St. Joseph Resident, **Shigeru Akabane** was born on July 5, 1941. Known professionally as Little Tokyo, he was a popular wrestler in the Midget Class. He once wrestled before a crowd of 93,000.

J.B. Shelton of Sulphur Springs caught a 200 pound gar on April 21, 1942. Inside he found an antique pocket watch, a silver fork, and a silver spoon.

On May 22, 1947, St. Louisan, **Erma Bergmann** threw a no hitter in the All American Girls Professional Baseball League. This is the league from the popular movie, *A League of Their Own.*

In what many regard as the greatest upset in World Cup history, the **U.S. team** beat England on June 5, 1950. Five of the players were from St. Louis and four of those were from "the Hill." A movie was made about the event. Much of *The Game of Their Lives* was filmed on the Hill.

Sonny Liston was born on May 8, 1932. He was one of 25 siblings. At age 18 he robbed a gas station and was sent to the state penitentiary at Jefferson City. There he learned prize fighting. He had only been boxing for eight months when, on March 26, 1953, he won the Golden Gloves heavyweight crown and in 1962 he knocked out Floyd Patterson to gain the World Championship.

St. Louis' **Dick Weber** held about every record imaginable in Bowling and was inducted into the Bowling Hall of Fame.

Kenny Schrader was born in St. Louis on May 25, 1955. He began his racing career on a go-kart in his yard and then moved up to the dirt track at Pevely. He went on to be one of the top drivers in the nation.

NASCAR owner, driver, broadcaster, **Rusty Wallace** was born on August 14, 1956 in Fenton, MO. His racing career began at the Lake Hill track in Valley Park. NASCAR star, Mike Wallace was born in Fenton, MO on March 10, 1959. On August 23, 1963 NASCAR star, Kenny Wallace was born in St. Louis. The Wallaces all went on to become racing legends.

What basketball star won state and national championships with St. Louis U. High School, St. Louis University, and the St. Louis Hawks in the NBA? **"Easy Ed" Macauley** earned All-Pro, and Hall of Fame honors.

On March 12, 1958, the **Budweiser Team** at Florissant Lanes bowled the highest score in bowling history. In three games they got a total score of 3858 pins.

The **Billikens at St. Louis University** won the national championship in soccer on November 29, 1959. The German, Italian, Irish, and other immigrant families make St. Louis a soccer hotbed. For this and other reasons the Billikens have been national champs in: 1960, 1962, 1963, 1965, 1967, 1969, 1970, 1972, and 1973. This is more national titles than any other school in America.

The **Christian Brothers Academy** (St. Louis) completed a 72-game undefeated streak in soccer on February 26, 1961.

How's this for a golf handicap? On June 19, 1954 pro golfer, **Ed Furgol**, of the Westwood Country Club won the U.S. Open. His left arm, injured in childhood, was ten inches shorter than his right arm.

Only one man has played for the Baseball Cardinals, the Football Cardinals, and the Blues. He played at Busch Stadium for the first time on April 15, 1972. **Ernie Hays** of course played the organ.

On February 15, 1978, St. Louisan, **Leon Spinks**, shocked the sports world when he beat Muhammed Ali in fifteen rounds for the World Heavyweight Crown. He and his brother, Michael, were the only brothers to ever hold world titles.

On July 8, 2000, *The Sporting News* named **St. Louis** the best sports town in America.

On November 10, 2001 **Kevin Thomas** of Sweet Springs shot a 33–point buck in Saline County.

From June 19, 2002 – July 3, 2002, **Steve Fossett** circumnavigated the globe in 13 days, 8 hours, 33 minutes (14 days, 19 hours, 50 minutes to landing) and 20,626.48 statute miles by himself in the balloon, *Spirit of Freedom.* Usually operating out of St. Louis, Fossett set 116 records in various sports.

In St. Louis, Circus Flora star, **Aleysa Gulevich**, set a World Record by spinning 107 hula hoops at the same time. This was on June 15, 2009.

Emily Beaver was a senior at Missouri State University and a runner on the Bears track team. On May 15, 2013, she went to the Plaster Sports Complex and tried for the record in jogging while juggling. Keeping three bean bags in the air she jogged around the track four times in 5 minutes, 58.17 seconds thus setting a new World Record for joggling.

Somersaulting is a fun but dangerous pastime. On November 9, 2013 a group of 865 people calling themselves the **Barrelrollman Organization**, met on Art Hill in St. Louis and set a new World Record by simultaneously somersaulting down the steep slope.

Many of us would be happy to run a full marathon in 5 hours, 48 minutes, and 28 seconds. On October 20, 2013, **David Babcock** of Warrensburg did this and set a World Record because he was knitting a scarf at the same time. The scarf he wove while running was more than 12 feet long!

Arrowhead Stadium is officially the loudest in the N.F.L. On October 13, 2013, the sound of the crowd was measured at 137.5 decibels in the closing minutes of a game. Bring your earplugs and have fun!

Missouri's Best . . .
(Scientist, Inventors, & Innovators)

Dr. John S. Sappington, physician, and <u>medical pioneer</u> from Franklin and Arrow Rock, MO was born on May 15, 1776. He developed a <u>medicine to control malaria</u> fever.

John James Audubon ended his business partnership in Ste. Genevieve when Ferdinand Rozier bought out his interests. This was on April 6, 1812. Audubon's share of the business brought him the equivalent of $120,000 in today's terms. This allowed Audubon the time and money to work full time as an <u>ornithologist.</u>

On June 5, 1822 **Samuel T. Hawken** arrived in St. Louis to begin making his famous Hawken's Rifles – the favorite of mountain men and pioneers.

St. Louis Doctor, **William Beaumont** was born on November 21, 1795. On April 25, 1853, he found Alexis St. Martin, who had suffered a huge stomach wound. Beaumont tended to the wound and studied the digestive system through the hole. By doing this, Beaumont learned a great deal of what we know today about our digestion. The patient lived a very long life and medical knowledge was greatly advanced.

Legendary botanist, naturalist and medical doctor, **Dr. George Engelmann**, was born on February 2, 1089. He came to Missouri on February 20, 1833. And for over forty years, his weather observations were the only records that anyone kept. He was also the primary developer of Henry Shaw's Gardens. He did most of the work in establishing what is now known as the Missouri Botanical Garden for Henry Shaw.

January 29, 1826 was the birthday of **John Thomas Hodgen**, pioneering surgeon, physician and inventor of several medical devices still used today. He taught and practiced medicine in St. Louis.

Joseph J. Lawrence was born on January 28, 1836. He developed a surgical disinfectant which he named Listerine. His friend, Jordan Lambert helped to perfect the formula and then founded a firm to market the liquid.

Edward Mallinkrodt was born on January 21, 1845. With his brothers, he used the family farm in St. Louis County to start the first chemical manufacturing firm west of the Mississippi.

October 13, 1854 was the birthday of **Doctor Augustus Charles Bernays**. Bernays was a medical pioneer who was the first Missouri doctor to successfully operate on a gunshot wound, perform a successful Caesarian section, and the first organ surgery.

Susan Blow was born in Carondolet (St. Louis), Missouri in 1843 to a family of great wealth and social standing. At age 27 she traveled to Germany and encountered what they termed a garden for growing little children or a kindergarten. She brought the idea of this transitional year and its special teaching methods back to American and established the first public kindergarten in the Des Peres School in Carondolet in 1873. Soon she had thirty kindergartens operating and the movement spread across the nation. She also established a special college to train kindergarten teachers. Today that school is known as the Harris-Stowe State College.

Henry Tibbe of Washington, Missouri patented an improved corncob pipe on July 9, 1878. Ever tried to make a corncob pipe? They burn up! Tibbe put just enough plaster of Paris in his pipe to make it hold the burning tobacco but still draw air creating a cool smoke. These "Missouri Meerschaums" are still manufactured on the riverfront in Washington.

The engineer, **James Buchanan Eads** is famous for doing what people said was impossible. He's the man who built Eads Bridge even though everyone said the Mississippi was way to wide and too powerful. He pioneered use of the diving bell, built armored gunboats for the Mississippi River Campaign, and much more.

January 10, 1864 is the probable birth date of **George Washington Carver** in Diamond, MO. On October 8, 1896 Carver taught his first class at Tuskegee Institute. Born a slave, this scientist probably saved the economy of the south with his concept of crop rotation and the hundreds of new products he developed from legumes. He died January 5, 1943.

On January 20, 1886, **William Burroughs** and three other men founded the Arithometer Company in St. Louis on this date. They were selling their new invention, the adding machine.

John Queeny was a buyer for a wholesale drug company but in 1901 he opened a small facility in St. Louis to manufacture artificial sweetener. He named the company after his wife, Olga Monsanto Queeny.

J.C. Penney As he grew up in Hamilton, MO Penney's parents stressed the Golden Rule and he put that theme into practice as a merchant. Known as "The Golden Rule Merchant," Penney operated hundreds of "dry goods" stores across the country. He was an innovator because his stores featured an established price with no bickering. He insisted that a good product for the customer and a fair profit for him was the way to do business and, with this policy he thrived.

Elmer F. Pierson was born in Kansas City on August 27, 1896. He and his brother, John, founded the Vendo Company, maker of the first reliable Coca-Cola vending machines. For years they dominated the vending machine industry.

Peanut Butter

Missouri-born **George Washington Carver** is often given credit for inventing peanut butter in 1903 but that is a mistake. He was a great agronomist and inventor and he did develop over 300 uses for the peanut. Because of his work, the entire agricultural economy of the south was saved so clearing up the record on peanut butter does not detract from Carver's accomplishments.

Peanut butter as we know it today was developed by a St. Louis physician (probably **Dr. George A Bayle, Jr.**) as a dietary supplement for his elderly patients who had no teeth. This was in 1890. Then in 1903, **Dr. Ambrose Straub**, also of St. Louis, patented a machine for making peanut butter. In 1904, another St. Louis resident, **C. H. Sumner**, introduced peanut butter to the general population when he sold it at his St. Louis World's Fair concession stand.

William Lear was born in Hannibal on June 26, 1902. Starting by charging batteries for 25 cents he went on to invent the car radio which he called a Motorola. (Motor Victrola) He also invented the eight-track music system and the Lear Jet.

Aaron "Bunny" Lapin was born in St. Louis on January 5, 1914. During WWII rationing he invented an oil substitute for whipped cream and called it Reddi-wip. He was also the first to market shaving cream in aerosol cans. Of course he made it squirt out of a can. Since then, we have enjoyed spray paint, silly string, and much more.

Charles Stark Draper was born in Windsor, MO on October 2, 1901. Draper invented the inertial navigation system which controls the flight of aircraft and spacecraft.

On January 24, 1922, a school teacher and candy store owner, **Christian Nelson**, got his patent on ice cream dipped in chocolate. The treats were manufactured by a candy maker in Kansas City, Mr. Russell Stover. They were called "I-Scream Bars" but we know them as Eskimo Pies.

January 17, 1927 was the birthday of medical doctor and humanitarian **Dr. Thomas Dooley** in St. Louis. He was a diligent medical pioneer in Southeast Asia and John F. Kennedy named Dooley as his inspiration for starting the Peace Corps.

John Robert Gregg was born in Ireland on February 23, 1948. He moved to St. Louis where he published something he called *Gregg Shorthand* which is the shorthand system still used today.

One of Missouri's most interesting characters was **Annie Malone**. Fluctuating between the extremes of poverty and wealth, Annie Malone helped thousands of African-Americans along the way. She was an inventor, entrepreneur, educator, and philanthropist. Some say that she was America's first black millionaire.

Hubert "Hub" Schlafly was born in St. Louis on August 14, 1919. In 1950 he invented the teleprompter to help soap opera actors. It soon became the politician's best friend.

Holless Wilbur Allen had been experimenting for years with block and tackle rigs and on June 23, 1966 the mechanic patented his new invention – the compound hunting bow. H. W. Allen was from Kansas City and Billings, MO.

The Hubble Telescope was launched into space on April 25, 1990. It was named for Marshfield-born astronomer, **Edwin Hubble**. (born 11-20-1889) Hubble changed almost everything we know about space. He discovered that most of the stars we see are not stars but galaxies each containing millions of stars. He found that the universe was expanding and learned how to measure the speed of movement. He was one of the two greatest modern <u>astronomers</u>.

In Jefferson City, **Jack Kilby** was born on November 8, 1923. He grew up to invent the integrated circuit and changed the lives of every American.

Jack Dorsey who grew up in St. Louis and went to school at the Missouri University of Science and Technology, started a little telephone network on March 1, 2006. It was a service for dispatching couriers. He calls it Twitter.

Missouri's Best . . .
(Pioneers & Explorers)

Pierre Marquette

June 1, 1637 was the birthday of Pierre Marquette, one of the two explorers who named Missouri. (Marquette and Joliet)

Father James Gravier

On October 10, 1700, a French missionary, Father James Gravier, noted in his journal, "Discovered the river Mirameguoua, where the rich lead mine is situated, 12 or 13 leagues from its mouth." Today we refer to that river as the Meramec. "Meramec" (Mirameguoua) is an Osage word meaning "catfish." The next day Father Gravier wrote of killing a buffalo below the mouth of a river he had described the previous day. This is the first record of white men in what is today Jefferson County.

Rene Auguste Chouteau

September 7, 1749 was the birthday of Rene August Chouteau. His father abandoned the family and poor Auguste would probably never amount to anything. But by age 14 he had founded the city of St. Louis and became one of the most influential men in history.

Madame Chouteau

Madame Chouteau, was the wife of the founder of St. Louis. The first "white" woman in St. Louis. Because of this, she was very important in the early development of the community. Her grandson founded Kansas City in 1821.

Francois Chouteau

Francois Chouteau was born on February 17, 1797. He is known as the "Father of Kansas City." In 1821 he established a trading post just east of what is now downtown. After a flood he moved to what is today the downtown area.

Charles Claude de Tisne

On November 22, 1719, Charles Claude de Tisne completed the first overland trek across what is now Missouri. This man led a small party up the Missouri River to meet with the Missouria and the Osage. Then he traveled south and west to meet the Wichita. They refused to let him go farther west so he returned overland across southern Missouri to Fort de Chartes. This was all more than eighty years before Lewis and Clark but de Tisne is seldom mentioned in our history books.

Daniel Boone:

A true legend, Daniel Boone was born in 1734. Boone and the people he brought may have done as much as any other people to give Missouri its unique and distinct character. On June 11, 1800 the Spanish government appointed Boone Commandant or "Syndic" of the Femme Osage District and granted him 850 acres plus 650 acres more for each family who came with him to Missouri. Boone settled near present day Defiance.

Daniel, his friends, and his sons settled the Missouri River Valley, especially on the north side and built beautiful homes. Many of those homes remain today. They enjoyed "long hunts" across the territory and maintained a second home at Ash Grove and established salt-making site at Boone's Lick

Daniel Boone died on September 26, 1820 at his home on the Femme Osage, near Defiance, MO. He and Rebecca were buried on a hilltop a short distance from their home and a monument was set in place.

Daniel Boone: (Continued)

Then in 1845 the state of Kentucky demanded that the bodies of Daniel and Rebecca be sent back for burial there. Family members objected and a court battle ensued. Kentucky won and the exhumation was ordered. Family members still argued that Boone was angry with Kentucky and left specific directions for his burial near Defiance.

On June 17, 1845, a group arrived in St. Charles County to take Daniel and Rebecca Boone's remains back for burial in Kentucky. One month later the group left with two bodies. Rumor had it that the family pointed out the wrong grave sites to the Kentuckians. In 1983, Forensic anthropologists and personal testimony indicated that the bones in the Frankfort, KY grave are not those of Daniel Boone.

Nathan Boone

As his father, Daniel, grew older, Nathan began to assume leadership on the American Frontier. He was probably the most influential and important person west of St. Louis. His salt lick and the area around it became the place for much of the settlement along the Missouri. By June 18, 1812 when the War of 1812 began, the tension had grown as relations between the various Europeans and the various Native nations shifted. Nathan Boone and others formed military units. This stabilized the frontier and pioneers continued to arrive in the great valley.

Louis Lorimier

On November 23, 1803, Lewis and Clark were still making their way toward St. Louis when they arrived at Cape Girardeau. Lewis was the dinner guest of the pioneer, Louis Lorimier. Clark was not welcome. Lewis noted that there was also a group of "duch" (German) settlers who had already erected mills and a group of about 400 Shawnee.

Clark was not welcome in Lorimier's home because, years earlier, his older brother, George Rogers Clark, had burned Lorimier's trading post and run him out of Ohio. This was because of the actions of Lorimier and his Shawnee allies during the French and Indian War. The 400 Shawnee came with Lorimier to Missouri. While in Missouri the Shawnee were operating ferry boats and other small businesses.

Henry Schoolcraft

Henry Schoolcraft was born on March 28, 1793. In addition to being an expert on Native Americans, he was the first white person to explore the Ozarks in depth.

Saint Rose Philippine Duchesne

Mother Rose Philippine Duchesne and her Order of the Sacred Heart opened a school on April 6, 1825. It was the first Catholic school for Indian girls in the United States. It was on the Bishop's farm located north of Florissant. She was the leader of the order that did much to establish schools for Native Americans and Girls on the frontier.

William Henry Ashley

Along with many discoveries and feats, William Henry Ashley is remembered as the person who created the idea of the yearly rendezvous system for mountain men and Indians. He did much to create the fur trade between the far west and St. Louis and made many discoveries during his life. He died on March 26, 1838 at his home in Boonville.

Father Pierre-Jean DeSmet

Father Pierre-Jean DeSmet, a beloved priest was born on January 30, 1801. He is remembered for his work with Native Americans in Missouri and was greatly respected by them. The Natives called him "Blackrobe"

Moses and Steven Austin

Moses Austin was born in 1761. A miner, developer of towns, leader in early Missouri, he left one day and rode to Mexico City hoping for an audience with the Emperor. He offered to bring Missourians to settle the area called Texas and the Emperor agreed. However, he died in Potosi before being able to finish his task and his son Steven Austin took the leadership role. Steven is known now as "The Father of Texas."

On April 22, 1938 the City of Potosi defeated the state of Texas. Texas filed papers to remove the body of Moses and place it in a Texas hero's grave. Potosi resisted. Today Moses Austin is still buried at his Memorial in Potosi.

Lewis and Clark:

On May 14, 1804 the Lewis and Clark Expedition (the Voyage of Discovery) left St. Louis to explore the unknown west. Thomas Jefferson had designed the expedition even before the area was purchased by the U.S. He directed Lewis & Clark to collect all sorts of scientific information, to look for a passage to the Pacific Ocean, and to establish good relations with the Sioux and others in the west.

Missouri's first superstar, William Clark, was born August 1, 1770. He was a leader of the Lewis and Clark Expedition, then appointed Governor of Missouri Territory and Director of Indian Affairs. He was the rock solid trusted leader of the expedition and the information he collected in his journeys were invaluable to scientists, planners and leaders in North America and Europe. He is buried in Bellefontaine Cemetery in St. Louis.

Explorer and naturalist, Meriwether Lewis was born on August 18, 1774. He lived in St. Louis while he acted as the first Governor of the Louisiana Territory. Lewis may have been the most intelligent member of the Corps of Discovery and was certainly the best educated. His insights were incredible and his discoveries were numerous. However, he may have suffered from Bi-Polar Syndrome which was an unknown ailment at the time. His best friend, President Jefferson, described him as having "fits of melancholy".

Lewis and Clark: (Continued)

During the expedition both officers and the rest of the crew performed almost flawlessly although Lewis did have some lapses in judgment. He was also unable to present his journals to the President as requested and required. Finally, while Lewis was living in St. Louis and supposedly completing his journals for submission, Jefferson summoned him to Washington where Lewis might get help with finishing his project.

On the trip to Washington Lewis mysteriously died at an inn in Tennessee. Some reports say that he was murdered and others report that he was depressed and shot himself. Either way, it was a sad end for a brilliant explorer.

The Expedition generated reports across the world of the great resources and the unparalleled adventure waiting west of the Mississippi and adventurers flooded in. Gateway cities like St. Louis, Westport, Kansas City, Weston, St. Joseph and Independence began to spring up and grow. The history of the world changed when Lewis & Clark returned from one of the greatest adventures since the beginning of time.

Manuel Lisa

Born on September 8 1772, Lisa became the leading fur trader in the Missouri Territory and did a great deal of exploring in the Rocky Mountains. On April 19, 1807 he started up the Missouri with 42 men. They founded Fort Raymond at the confluence of the Yellowstone and the Big Horn and gave all future explorers an outpost in the wilderness.

John Colter

Selected as a hunter for the Voyage of Discovery, Colter was soon recognized as one of the stars of the Expedition. As Lewis & Clark returned home by one route they allowed Colter to go in a different direction. He discovered what came to be known as "Colter's Hell" and what today we call the Yellowstone National Park.

After escaping from the Blackfoot Indians who were hunting him for sport, he returned to Missouri and purchased some farm land he had spotted as the Expedition first traveled westward. This land is near present day New Haven, MO. He married an Osage woman and they raised a large family which holds annual reunions at New Haven to this day.

John C. Fremont

Military officer and explorer (known as the Great Pathfinder), John C. Fremont was born on January 21, 1813. He was a leader (along with Kit Carson) of several expeditions west and more responsible than anyone else for America's possession of California. On November 26, 1848 the Great Pathfinder, along with "Old Bill" Williams and other Missourians chose the wrong pass and became stranded in a severe Rocky Mountain winter. At one point the men thought they saw green grass in the snow. It turned out to be the tops of evergreen trees. Eleven men died on that trip and Old Bill was accused of cannibalism.

On July 3, 1861, Fremont was appointed Commander of the Western Department of the Army headquartered at Jefferson City. Lincoln chastised him for freeing the slaves in Missouri and he then called Lincoln an imbecile. On September 11, 1861, President Lincoln revoked John C. Fremont's emancipation proclamation for Missouri slaves.

Jedediah Smith

June 24, 1798 was the birthday of the legendary explorer and mountain man, Jedediah Smith.

Ann Hawkins Gentry

Born on January 21, 1791, the pioneering Ann Hawkins Gentry of Columbia began a significant life. She was the wife of soldier and adventurer, Richard Gentry, mother of thirteen children, and widowed in war, she was only the second woman in American history to serve as a postmistress (which she did for 27 years in Columbia).

William Ashley

On April 3, 1822, William Ashley and one hundred "enterprising young men" left St. Louis for the Upper Missouri and the Rockies. They were to establish a fur trading operation. This group included Jim Bridger, Bill Sublette, Jedediah Smith, and others who would become mountain man legends. Ashley was from Ste. Genevieve and was known as a good leader of men. He died on March 26, 1838 in Boonville

Jean Baptiste Charbonneau:

Jean Baptiste Charbonneau, the son of Toussaint Charbonneau and Sacajawea was born at the Mandan Indian camp on the Upper Missouri on February 11, 1805. Kirkwood author, Anna Lee Waldo tells us that, to hasten her baby's birth, Sacajawea was given a tea made from rattles taken from the giant snakes collected by Meriwether Lewis in the cave at St. Alban, Missouri. After going as an infant on the Voyage of Discovery with Lewis and Clark, he came to St. Louis for his education.

He came with his parents in 1807 to St. Louis and they went west again in 1809 leaving Jean Baptiste with William Clark so he could get a good education. Records show that Clark was busy on January 22, of 1820 making arrangements and paying for the schooling of Jean Baptiste. He attended the St. Louis Academy which today is called St. Louis University High School. The school was located in the storehouse of Joseph Robidoux.

By March 31, 1820, William Clark's wife had said that Jean Baptiste could not live with them so Clark was out arranging for and paying for lodging, meals, and laundry for the child. Records show that April 1 was another shopping day for William Clark and Jean Baptiste. Clark bought the boy a slate and pencils, schoolbooks, and clothing.

Jean Baptiste Charbonneau: (Continued)

Eventually Jean Baptiste was well educated and old enough to strike out on his own. He had already known the adventure of traveling on the Lewis and Clark Expedition and living among the Native Americans and the people of the St. Louis settlement but he wanted more adventure. He went west in 1823.

It was October 9, 1823 when he met The Duke of Wurtemburg and the Duke invited Jean Baptiste to travel with him back to Europe. This would be the second of many adventures for Sacajawea's son. He traveled throughout Europe the explored in Africa, the Carribbean, and eventually returned to St. Louis. From there he returned to the western frontier. Some of his companions on the frontier were Jim Bridger, James Beckwourth, and John C. Fremont.

In all, he probably had more adventures in his life than anyone other than Marco Polo but, because he didn't like the limelight, many people are not familiar with his story. Did you know that Jean Baptiste Charbonneau was the only child ever to be depicted on a United States coin?

Joseph Robidoux

Joseph Robidoux was born August 10, 1783. At age 16, he established Fort Dearbon Trading Post (now known as Chicago, IL) the in 1826 he established the Blacksnake Hills Trading Post which we know today as St. Joseph, Missouri.

Louis Rubidoux

July 31, 1796 was the birthday of St. Louis born, Louis Rubidoux. He was a French-Canadian fur trapper and explorer who opened up New Mexico and California to American settlement. He is not believed to be related to Joseph Robidoux.

Zebulon Pike

On July 15, 1806, Zebulon Pike left St. Louis on a journey of exploration of the southwestern Louisiana Purchase area. He probably didn't know that he was a part of a treasonous plot to separate that part of the territory from the United States. At any rate, he was an important explorer and his accomplishments have been recognized by naming many things in his honor including Pike County, Missouri.

William Becknell

It was a historic day on September 1, 1821 when frontiersman, William Becknell, began his first trip on what would become the Santa Fe Trail. This soldier, politician, trailblazer, and freight operator from St. Charles and Arrow Rock opened the lucrative trade of the Southwest (then Mexico) to America.

George Sibley

George Sibley and his party departed from St. Charles on June 27, 1825 to survey what would become the Santa Fe Trail. Prior to that he had been the "Factory" meaning the person who operated Fort Bellefountaine and Fort Osage Trading Posts. He was one of the most trusted men among the Native Americans. His St. Charles home named Linden Wood was the start of an early school which became Lindenwood University.

Russell, Majors, & Waddell:

William H. Russell (b. 1-31-1812) from Lexington, Alexander Majors (b. 10-4-1814) from Westport, and William B. Waddell (b. 10-14-1807) from Lexington were incredibly important in the opening of America's West. They are well-known for their founding of the Overland Stage Company and the Pony Express.

William H. Russell (b. 1-31-1812) from Lexington, Alexander Majors (b. 10-4-1814) from Westport, and William B. Waddell (b. 10-14-1807) from Lexington were incredibly important in the opening of America's West. They are well-known for their founding of the Overland Stage Company and the Pony Express.

With more than three thousand wagons in operation, they employed better than four thousand people. They also used over forty thousand oxen and more than ten thousand mules. The wagons took manufactured goods to the far west and brought minerals, furs, and more to the markets which were accessible by steamboats from Missouri.

These men also founded a mail service to connect the new nation's east and west. Of course that was the Pony Express. Russell, Majors, and Waddell enabled commerce and provided safety and prosperity for the western territories along the Santa Fe Trail, the Oregon Trail, and everywhere in between.

Jedediah Smith

June 24, 1798 was the birthday of the legendary explorer and mountain man, Jedediah Smith.

Jim Bridger

Mountain man, Jim Bridger was born on March 17, 1804. He made many discoveries in the west and established Fort Bridger which was an extremely important outpost for westward pioneers. Prior to his adventures he had been a farmer near present day Kansas City. He died on July 17, 1881 at his home in Kansas City, MO.

Kit Carson

Christopher "Kit" Carson from Franklin, MO, was born on Christmas Eve, 1809. He did as much as any person to open up the west. He was an explorer, trapper, guide, interpreter, and eventually General in the US Army. For an idea of his importance, look at a map of the U.S. and see how many places are named for him, as in Carson City, Carson Mountain, Carson County, etc.

William Ray

William Ray was born on January 18, 1808. He is important to history because he operated a blacksmith shop on the Santa Fe Trail in a spot which is today named for him - Raytown. He not only helped many local farmers who were settling in western Missouri, but he got people ready for their journeys westward toward the Oregon Territory.

John Butterfield

John Butterfield was born on November 18, 1801. He founded the Butterfield Overland Mail stage line from St. Louis to San Francisco. He also founded American Express.

Ben Holladay

Ben Holladay, known as the "Stagecoach King," was born on October 14, 1819. This Weston resident, famous for his stagecoach line was also the founder of the McCormick Distillery.

Thomas Lawson Price

Thomas Lawson Price, born January 19, 1809, was the first mayor of Jefferson City and the owner of the first stage coach line between St. Louis and Jefferson City. He was also the part-owner and developer of several Missouri railroads.

John O'Fallon

Philanthropist John O'Fallon was born on November 23, 1791. He established the O'Fallon Institute which is now Washington University. He built and donated new buildings to St. Louis University. He also started and served as the first president for three important railroads. Many things today including O'Fallon, Missouri are named for him.

Sisters of Mercy

On March 1, 1871, the Sisters of Mercy came from Ireland to open St. John's Infirmary in St. Louis. This was the beginning of all of the Mercy Medical Centers across the state. They also founded many fine schools in Missouri.

Calamity Jane

Martha Jane Cannary Burke was born in Princeton, MO on May Day, 1852. She loved the life of adventure and spent much of her life in the rugged west. The pretty young woman was once approached by some soldiers who were flirting with her. She warned them that to court her was "to court calamity." From that day forward Martha Jane became known as "Calamity Jane."

Calamity Jane

Buffalo Bill Cody

Young William F. Cody had spent a good deal of his youth in Weston, Missouri following the death of his father. In Weston he worked at his uncle's general hardware store. On March 6, 1866 Cody married Louisa Frederici in St. Louis. The next year Cody left Missouri to hunt buffalo providing meat for workers on the Kansas Pacific Railroad. He claimed to have killed 4,280 buffalo during that 17 month period and became well-known as "Buffalo Bill."

In the 1890s, Buffalo Bill operated a very popular Wild West Show. Because of Louisa, Cody's Wild West Show was, for many years based in St. Louis. Because of this fact, Annie Oakley, Buffalo Bill, Geronimo, and others could sometimes be seen in St. Louis preparing for their next show. Buffalo Bill Cody's Wild West Show used to spend their winters on a race track in North St. Louis.

Former Pony Express Rider, Buffalo Bill Cody helping to dedicate the Pony Express Monument in St. Joseph.

Captain Ashley McKinley & Ensign Thomas Mulroy

Two St. Louisans, Captain Ashley McKinley and Ensign Thomas Mulroy, were with Rear Admiral Richard E. Bird as he explored the Polar Regions. The three of them dedicated the St. Louis Flying Field as the Lambert-St. Louis Municipal Airport on July 12, 1930.

Steve Fossett

On July 2, 2002, the adventurer Steve Fossett, traveled non-stop around the world in fourteen days in his hot air balloon. Bush Stadium in St. Louis was his favorite launch site and Washington University in St. Louis was his mission control. Fossett held 116 records in various fields.

The **Tier One** project, using the experimental space plane SpaceShipOne, won the X PRIZE on October 4, 2004. The X PRIZE space competition, announced in 1996, was meant to spur new thinking about low-cost space flight. The X PRIZE Foundation, based in St. Louis and inspired by the example of Charles Lindbergh, offered a $10 million prize for the first nongovernmental organization to launch a reusable manned spacecraft into space twice within two weeks.

Spaceship One

Tom Akers

On May 20, 1951, astronaut Tom Akers was born in St. Louis, Missouri. He grew up in Eminence, Missouri and graduated from Eminence High School. He received a Bachelor of Science degree and a Master of Science degree in Applied Mathematics from the University of Missouri-Rolla in 1973 and 1975, respectively and eventually Colonel Akers made four trips into space. On October 6, 1990, Akers lifted off for the first time.

Astronaut Tom Akers

Linda M. Godwin

Astronaut Linda M. Godwin lifted off on the first of her four trips into space on April 5, 1991. She was born in Cape Girardeau on July 2, 1952 and grew up in Jackson. She graduated from Jackson H.S., Southeast Missouri State U., and the University of Missouri before becoming an astronaut. She received a Bachelor of Science degree in <u>Mathematics</u> and <u>Physics</u> from <u>Southeast Missouri State University</u> in 1974, and a Master of Science degree and a Doctorate in <u>Physics</u> from the <u>University of Missouri</u>.

Astronaut Linda M. Godwin

Janet Lynn Kavandi

Janet Lynn Kavandi was born January 17 in Carthage, MO. Kavandi graduated from <u>Carthage Senior High School</u>, <u>Missouri Southern State College</u>, and the <u>Missouri University of Science and Technology</u>. On June 2–12, 1998, she took off on the first of her three missions into space. She orbited the earth a total of 535 times.

Astronaut Janet Lynn Kavandi

Astronaut Mike Hopkins

On September 25, 2013, Astronaut Mike Hopkins was launched into space to serve aboard the Soyuz Space Station. Mike was born in Lebanon, MO on December 28, 1968 and he grew up on a farm near Richland, MO. He graduated from the School of the Osage in Lake Ozark, Missouri then went to Univ. of Illinois & Stanford U. At this writing, he is still aboard the Space Station on his first flight.

Astronaut Mike Hopkins

Missouri's Best . . .
(Arts & Entertainment)

George Caleb Bingham

Perhaps Missouri's greatest artist, George Caleb Bingham from Franklin, Arrow Rock, and St. Louis, MO, was born on March 20, 1811. Without his rich and accurate paintings, we might not know so much about life in early Missouri. Starting as a struggling artist and working as a custodian in his mother's school, he went on to create paintings worth countless millions of dollars.

Laura Ingalls Wilder

Though, born in Malone, NY and living in places like Minnesota and Kansas, Laura had not written down any of her stories. Then while working at the library in Mansfield, MO, people encouraged her to write down her childhood stories. Published first in magazines and then in several extremely popular books, she became one of America's favorite writers.

She and Almonzo worked hard on their farm (Rocky Ridge Ranch) and local newspapers often carried stories of outstanding corn and other crops they had grown. One told of a ten pound radish from their garden. But she will always be known for the inspiring stories of life in her little cabins and finally in her big farm home.

Rocky Ridge Ranch in Mansfield
Home of Laura Ingalls Wilder

Vinnie Ream

The very talented sculptress from Christian College in Columbia, Vinnie Ream, at age 18 was given the commission by Congress to sculpt the statue of Abraham Lincoln to stand in the Nation's Capital Rotunda. The famous statue was unveiled on January 25, 1871.

Thomas Hart Benton

One of Missouri's two greatest artists, Thomas Hart Benton, was born in Neosho on April 15, 1889. His paintings and sculptures are found in every major art museum. Luckily for us, many of his best originals are available to us in Kansas City, St. Louis, the State Historical Society (Columbia), and throughout the state's Capital Building.

Margaret Brown

Hannibal's Maggie Brown was not actually an entertainer but she was the inspiration for some terrific books, Broadway plays, and a very popular movie. She led an extremely interesting life which was made famous as The Unsinkable Molly Brown.

Samuel Clemens

Clemens, who wrote under the name of Mark Twain, was born in Florida, MO and moved with his family to Hannibal at a very young age. Hannibal was Missouri's second largest city and a very exciting river port. He fulfilled his dream and got his riverboat pilot's license in 1859 but went west when the Civil War broke out.

After writing newspaper articles and short stories, in 1885 he published *Adventures of Huckleberry Finn*. This book has been described as the definitive work of American literature and the work by which all others were to be measured. Of course he published many other terrific books and stories all the rest of his life.

Rose O'Neill

Branson's Rose O'Neill was an artist and illustrator who created the kewpie doll which was popular for many decades. The kewpie is still often seen as a stereotypical angel.

Scott Joplin

Growing up and getting his education in the roughest part of a rough cattle town (Sedalia), Scott Joplin discovered early in life that he had a talent for music. He wrote music in a new kind of jazz called ragtime and performed in the saloons of Sedalia, St. Louis and other cities. Soon he was dubbed "The King of Ragtime." In 1903, the largest selling sheet music was Scott Joplin's "*The Entertainer*." It would be number one again decades later after the movie "*The Sting*." If you can create something that remains popular for over 100 years, you've done something right.

Eugene Field

"The Children's Poet" was born in St. Louis on September 2, 1850. He authored many of the poems which became a part of millions of children's childhoods. On December 18, 1936, his home opened as a toy museum. It is still a popular tourist attraction and stands on Broadway near the new Busch Stadium.

Harold Bell Wright

Harold Bell Wright who wrote *The Shepherd of the Hills* and 18 other novels was born on May 4, 1872. Two were made into movies starring Gary Cooper and John Wayne. He served as a Christian minister in Pierce City and Lebanon, MO. Wright's novel, *The Calling of Dan Matthews*, is the story of his experiences in Lebanon. It gives a good picture of life in a small rural town in Missouri at the turn of the century. One of his characters, The Printer of Udell, was said by Ronald Reagan to be an important inspiration in his life.

Sara Teasdale

The lyrical poet, Sara Teasdale, was born in St. Louis on August 8, 1884. She was born Sara Trevor Teasdale and after her marriage in 1914 she went by the name Sara Teasdale Filsinger

Vance Randolph

Pineville, Missouri's great folklorist, Vance Randolph was born on February 23, 1892 and his tales of the Ozarks still delight people today.

Cliff Edwards

Cliff Edwards was born in Hannibal on April 25, 1895 and became somewhat famous as "Ukulele Ike" in St. Louis saloons. When he died in 1971, Edwards' body went unclaimed for several days because nobody knew who he was. However this old entertainer had played in more than 100 movies and had done voice-overs for many characters including Jiminy Cricket. His voice is the one that sang Disney's famous "When You Wish Upon a Star."

Walt Disney

Innovator with animated cartoons, theme parks, and more, Walt Disney from Marceline, and Kansas City, MO was born on December 5, 1901. Missouri's Secretary of State issued incorporation papers for Walt Disney's KC studio known as Laugh-O-Gram Films on May 23, 1922. On September 19, 1928, Disney introduced his Mickey Mouse character to the public at the Colony Theater on this day and the rest is history.

It's interesting to note that, as a boy, Walt Disney delivered newspapers for the Kansas City Star. Later he got a job working inside and writing for the paper. He was soon fired because of his complete lack of creativity. A few years later this creative genius bought the Kansas City Star!

Jean Harlow

The "Blonde Bombshell" was born in Kansas City on March 3, 1911. Harlean Harlow Carpenter changed her name to Jean Harlow and became the biggest sex symbol in Hollywood during the 1930s.

Ginger Rogers

America's sweetheart song and dance girl, Ginger Rogers hailed from Independence and Kansas City, Missouri. She was born on July 16, 1911.

Sally Benson

Sally Benson was born on September 3, 1900 in St. Louis. She wrote a series of autobio-graphical short stories for a magazine then compiled them into a book. This book became the basis for *Meet Me in St. Louis*. She went on to write other screenplays including *National Velvet*, *Bus Stop*, and *Anna and the King of Siam*. (*The King and I*)

Joyce Hall

As a boy, Joyce was working in a small town drug store as a boy when a salesman came in with a new product. It was called a picture post card. Those he had weren't very good and Joyce thought he could do better. He began taking pictures and having them put on good card stock and soon he tried making other kinds of cards. At his death he was worth $1.5 billion and was the founder of Hallmark Cards, the Hallmark Channel, Hallmark Hall of Fame, and more.

Mel Bay

Legendary musician, music producer, and instructor, Mel Bay, was born in Bunker, MO on February 25, 1913. He gained fame in St. Louis then in 1947 he began to produce something new – "how to" books for musicians from his facility in Pacific, MO. One can only guess how many millions of musicians learned to play with the "Mel Bay Method."

Robert Altman

Moviemaker, Robert B. Altman was born in Kansas City on February 20, 1925. He was educated in Kansas City and in the Wentworth Military Academy in Lexington. He made industrial films in KC before leaving for Hollywood.

Betty Grable

On March 30, 1931, the _Globe-Democrat_ reported that St. Louisan, Betty Grable seemed assured of "talkie stardom." She did go on to star in 42 films and was the most popular pin-up girl for the American G.I.s of World War II.

Red Foley

Many country western musicians and comedians owe their success in large measure to Red Foley. Himself a good musician, he started a nationally syndicated TV show in Springfield. The popular show was known as the Ozark Jubilee. It offered the first national stage to many of music's best entertainers.

Count Basie

August 21, 1904 was the Birthday of Kansas City's jazz great, William "Count" Basie. Because of Basie it was said that jazz was born in New Orleans but it grew up in Kansas City.

Marlon Perkins

Marlon Perkins was born in Carthage, MO on March 28, 1905. He was an effective and popular head of the St. Louis Zoo and his national television show, _"Wild Kingdom,"_ ran for 23 years. He was good at everything he did but is best remembered for saying things on TV like, "Just look at Jim wrestling that huge python! Hang on Jim!" Jim was probably saying things like, "Arghkrrrghkkgh!" as the python squeezed.

Porter Wagoner

Country music legend, Porter Wagoner, was born in West Plains on August 12, 1927. He worked for years in Springfield on Radio and TV.

Vincent Price

The handsome, frightening, and incredibly talented and versatile actor, Vincent Price, was born in St. Louis on May 27, 1911. Known as "the King of the Horror Movie," Vincent Price became a Hollywood legend.

Tennessee Williams

St. Louis' snobbish playwright, Tennessee Williams, was born on March 26, 1911. He wrote plays sometimes based on his life in that city. (The playwright's father was actually the one born in Tennessee.)

David Merrick

David Margulois was born in St. Louis on November 27, 1911. After changing his name to David Merrick he produced Hello Dolly, 42nd Street, Gypsy, and more. In all, his nearly 100 shows earned him eight Tony awards.

William Inge

William Inge was born on May 3, 1913. While working as a drama critic and an instructor at Washington University in St. Louis, he decided to write plays. Some of his work included *Bus Stop*, *Picnic*, and *Splendor in the Grass*.

Lanford Wilson

Hall of Fame playwright, Lanford Wilson was born on April 23, 1937. He grew up in Lebanon, Springfield, and Ozark, MO.

Chuck Berry

St. Louis' legendary musician Chuck Berry was born on October 18, 1926. In addition to his own hits, Berry wrote music for lots of groups including The Beach Boys and The Beatles. Paul McCartney said that, "If Rock and Roll didn't have a name, we'd have to call it Chuck Berry music."

Tina Turner

November 26, 1939 is the birthday of Tina Turner, the "High Priestess of Shout & Shimmy." The "Queen of Rock & Roll" had her roots in St. Louis.

Phyliss Diller

Possibly the funniest comedienne from Missouri, Phyliss Ada Driver was born on July 17, 1917. From her home in Webster Groves she performed and became a regular at the Gaslight Square where she was known as Phyliss Diller. She went on to fame with Bob Hope and others. And, yes, her husband, Fang, was also a Missourian.

Kay Thompson

Kay Thompson (a.k.a. Catherine Fink) was born in St. Louis on November 9, 1909. She wrote songs for motion pictures and stage shows but she is best remembered as a children's author. She wrote about the rambunctious six-year-old, *Eloise*.

Burt Bacharach

Musician-composer Burt Bacharach from Kansas City was born on May 12, 1928. He created some of the most popular music of the twentieth century.

Paul Henning

Producer, Paul Henning was born in Independence on September 16, 1911 and grew up on a farm near there. He worked as a writer for KMBZ Radio in Kansas City and would occasionally sing in their live music broadcasts. Eventually Henning left K.C. and wrote for *Fibber McGee & Molly*, *The Burns & Allen Show*, Green Acres, Petticoat Junction, and *The Bob Cummings Show*. Then, drawing on his memories of camping vacations near Branson, he created the *Beverly Hillbillies*. He even wrote the words and music for the theme song, *The Ballad of Jed Clampett*.

The Beatles

No! The Beatles were not from Missouri! However, they did spend more time than you probably realize in the Show-Me State. They played to huge crowds in the baseball stadiums of Kansas City (1964) and St. Louis (1966) but they also had a Missouri secret. In the Ozark Mountains near Alton (Oregon County) they had a place for relaxing, swimming, hiking, horse riding, go-karting, shooting and fishing. It was provided to them by a business associate from Missouri.

Mary Engelbreit

Mary Engelbreit was born in St. Louis on June 5, 1952 and soon had her "vast empire of cuteness." She was turned down by major publishers and artists so she eventually formed her own company. Englebreit has always been generous with her old high school, Visitation Academy.

Rush Limbaugh

Born in Cape Girardeau, Rush Limbaugh always wanted to work in the radio field. His first job was on the radio in that town where he used the name Rusty Sharpe. On August 1, 1988 the first national Rush Limbaugh Show aired and it revolutionized and revived talk radio.

Doris Roberts

The popular actress, Doris Roberts (Doris May Green) was born in St. Louis on November 4, 1925. She has played many rolls but is best known as Ray Barone's mother and Frank's "trophy wife" on *Everybody Loves Raymond*.

John Goodman

Actor and star of stage, screen, and television, John Goodman from Affton, MO was born on June 20, 1952.

Brad Pitt

Springfield's actor, hunk, and heartthrob, Brad Pitt was born on December 18, 1963.

Cedric the Entertainer

Cedric Antonio Kyles was born April 24, 1964 in Jefferson City. He grew up in Caruthersville and then Berkely, MO. He attended college at Southeast Missouri State University and, before his entertainment career took off, he worked as a substitute teacher. This writer would have loved having him as a substitute teacher!

Missouri's Worst . . .
(Villains, Outlaws & Dastardly Deeds)

James Wilkinson

The Territory of Louisiana was established with St. Louis as the seat of Government. James Wilkinson was the first Governor. On March 3, 1807, after being branded a traitor and spy, Governor Wilkinson was expelled from office. He served less than two years.

It turned out that Wilkinson was a close friend of Benedict Arnold and served as a double agent for the Spanish. He plotted with Aaron Burr to raise a Missouri army, separate the territory from the U.S. then conquer and rule Mexico.

Slickers

This terrible chapter in our history began with the feud between the Turk and Jones families from near Warsaw, MO. On election day in 1840 an argument erupted and charges were filed. Soon the eldest member of the Turk family was dead and a witness had disappeared. More trouble followed and soon a Turk "posse" was raiding the homes of anyone who supported the Jones or their allies.

The result of being caught by the Turks was a "slickering." This meant an extreme whipping with hickory switches. The purpose of the switches was to strip away the person's skin and flesh to allow severe (often fatal) bleeding and pain. The Slickers War spread to several Missouri counties and to distant Louisiana and Texas. Anti-Slickers Leagues were formed and the Governor had to mobilize the State Militia to put down the violence. The worst of the activities lasted from 1843 to 1845.

Slikering Prisoners

Frank James

Frank James was born in Clay County, MO (near Kearney). After a terrible series of events was inflicted upon his family, James joined Quantrill's Raiders and fought in the War Between the States. After the war he continued his campaign against the banks, railroads, and the U.S. Army. He and his brother, Jesse, basically invented the train robbery and robbed banks and other places with a flair.

The James-Younger Gang attempted a robbery of the bank at Northfield, Minnesota on September 7, 1876. At its conclusion only Frank and Jesse James were left alive and un-captured. James, on October 5, 1882, surrendered on the steps of the state capitol. He made a short speech and turned his gun over to the Governor. Later in life he held many positions including a race track commissioner and bouncer in a St. Louis theater.

William Quantrill

Civil war hero or villain (depending on your views) William Clarke Quantrill, of Quantrill's Raiders was born on July 31, 1837. Despised by many, Quantrill led a very successful band of Guerilla fighters that played havoc with Union forces.

Wm. Quantrill

Cole Younger

January 15, 1844 was the birthday in Jackson County of the Mayor of Harrisonville, farmer, guerilla fighter and outlaw, Cole Younger. A leading member of the Cole-Younger Gang, he became extremely hard to catch because of his relationship with Belle Starr who is said to have been in love with Younger.

On November 7, 1880, Cole Younger was being interviewed when he said, "The people of western Missouri are, in some respects, very peculiar. We will take Jackson County where I was born for instance. In that section the people seemed to be born fighters, the instinct being inherited from a long line of ancestors."

Cole Younger was paroled from prison on February 16, 1903 (after the botched Northfield, MN bank robbery) and returned to Missouri on that date. He met with Frank James in Kansas City and organized the "Buckskin Wild West Show.

Alf Bolin

In southern Missouri the people will say, "There weren't nuthin' good about Alf Bolin. He was lower than a snake in the rocks around Forsyth, Missouri. We know that he organized a gang of somewhere between twenty and fifty men who terrorized south Missouri. He claimed to be fighting for the Confederacy but it's probably closer to the truth to say that he was fighting against authority. He was just taking advantage of the fact that most of the able-bodied men were away from home and at the war.

There was a place that came to be called Bolin's Rocks or Murder Rocks. There, the gang ambushed people passing on the road below. He let nothing stop him. No one knows how many people he killed during his time along the Fox Creek but at least fourteen murders of old men, children, and women have been documented. He also killed at least two soldiers.

Finally a soldier named Zach Thomas went to the home of a family named Foster. Mr. Foster was a southern sympathizer and was a prisoner of war. Foster was promised a release if his family would help with the plan to get Alf Bolin. The Union soldier was disguised as a Confederate soldier and pretended to be sick as he stayed for several days hoping that Alf Bolin would appear. Eventually Bolin did come to the house and was hacked with a plowshare by the soldier. They took the body into another room only to discover that he was not dead. So they killed him again.

When they took the body to Forsyth a street celebration began. The good citizens decapitated Bolin and put the head on a pole in the center of Ozark, Missouri. This was on May 15, 1863. Since that time, people wanting to get married or looking for a good day to celebrate can choose to do so on what has been called Alf Bolin Day. May 15 is a charmed and lucky day in the Forsyth area!

There is one last part to this story. Since the gang was so active and pulled so many robberies, there is a story of loot hidden and marked with the skull of a horse. But only Bolin knew just where to look. Now treasure hunters continue to scour the area along Route JJ ten miles south of Forsyth near Gobbler's Knob. If someone finds that treasure it will be a good thing. Otherwise, there weren't nuthin' good about Alf Bolin.

Sam Hildebrand

The time of the War Between the States was a sad period in Missouri's history. You are reading about some of the human cockroaches who came out of the woodwork during that time. On November 25, 1863, Governor Fletcher called out the state militia to search for the man that some described as Missouri's most notorious outlaw. Samuel Hildebrand and his men had recently plundered Farmington and were known responsible for at least thirty murders! Or was he? Orville Turner of Richwoods, Missouri points out that the Union sympathizers called Hildebrand the Big River Bushwhacker a ruthless murderer but Confederate supporters called him a Rob Roy or a freedom fighter.

In 1861, a vigilante group lynched Sam's brother so Sam killed them. Then federal troops burned the family home and shot and killed several of his relatives – including his 13-year-old brother. Sam became a rebel guerrilla fighter and with his famous rifle, Kill-Devil, he declared his own war on the Union Army. It is said that he had 80 notches carved in the stock of his rifle.

Hildebrand died while resisting arrest in 1872 but he had dictated the story of his life to two newspaper men. In his own words he said, "I make no apology to mankind for my acts of retaliation; I make no whining appeal to the world for sympathy. I sought revenge and I found it; the key of hell was not suffered to rust in the lock while I was on the war path."

John Wilkes Booth

January 11, 1864 was one of his last appearances John Wilkes Booth performed in Shakespeare's *"Richard the III"* at the St. Louis Theater. Of course he soon after murdered President Lincoln.

Belle Starr

The "Bandit Queen" Belle Starr (Myra Maybelle Shirley) was born in Carthage, MO on February 3, 1846. She was probably the most infamous of all the pistol-packin' mamas of those days. She was notorious for helping outlaws evade capture. After she married an American-Indian outlaw and head of the Starr Clan in the Indian Territory, she had a home there where she offered safe haven and sanctuary for many men on the run.

Belle Starr

Jesse James & His Gang:

A simple explanation of Jesse James and his deeds just can't be accurate. The situation surrounding this gang's activities is very complicated and mysterious. Following the Civil War the group, more properly called the James-Younger Gang began to strike out at the railroads and banks who had made life miserable for their friends and neighbors. There was also some mysterious connection between the gang and the most prominent state politicians.

On September 26, 1872, the James Gang robbed the box office at the Kansas City Fair and right in the middle of a crowd of 10,000 people. The K.C. papers praised the outlaws for their daring. Why would newspapers praise the bandits? Jesse was known to commit a robbery and then give a hand-written press release to the victims so the details would be correctly reported in the newspapers.

The hated Pinkerton "detectives" were brought in by the railroad interests and on March 17, 1874, John Younger, of the James-Younger Gang was killed in a shootout with Pinkertons at Roscoe in St. Clair County, MO. It is claimed that the term "private eye" came from the all-seeing eye which forms the logo of the Pinkerton Agency. It is also claimed that these railroad detectives sent many innocent men to jail and thus, gave rise to the saying that a person had been "railroaded." At times Pinkerton detectives were little more than hired guns

In March of 1875 – The State Legislature was debating amnesty for the James and Younger brothers. Backers pointed out that they would have been called heroes if they had been on the Union side. But, after only two days of debate, the Legislature rejected the amnesty proposal.

Jesse James & His Gang: (Continued)

An odd report appeared in newspapers on April 16, 1880. Passengers reported that Jesse and Frank James traveled and ate lunch aboard the eastbound train between Kansas City and Odessa on this date. They reportedly ate with cocked revolvers on the table. On another trip they boarded a train and seemed interested in having lunch. But a brass band was returning home from a fair and, since they had their pay with them, they all wore guns. The James-Younger group decided to get off the train early.

Though Frank James, Cole Younger, and others from the gang held very public jobs in the end. The gang's activities came to a clear end on April 3, 1882 when Jesse James was shot dead by a gang member, Bob Ford at St. Joseph, Missouri. The Mayor of St. Joseph asked the governor to send the state militia to his city. It was feared that members of the James Gang would seek retribution for Jesse's death. But the gang was finished and nothing remained but the memories and the mysteries.

Frank & Jessie Prior to the Civil War

Wyatt Earp

In Dodge City, KS, they will tell you that Wyatt Earp was a hero. In fact, they have a larger-than-life bronze statue of the man on their main street. However, Missourians will know that he was an outlaw and a bully.

On March 14, 1871, Barton County, Missouri filed a lawsuit against Wyatt Earp claiming that he did not surrender the tax money and fees he had collected for local schools. That's right. He collected taxes for the schools then kept the money! Then, on March 28, 1871, he and two other men were each charged with stealing two horses. Nine days later a Deputy US Marshall arrested Earp for the theft.

On March 31, 1871, James Cromwell filed a lawsuit against Earp in Barton County claiming that Earp had filed false papers and withheld money owed to Cromwell. Finally, on June 5, 1871, Wyatt Earp, waiting to go on trial in Barton County for horse stealing, climbed through the roof of the jail and skipped the state. Good riddance!

The Gunn City Massacre

In Cass County on April 24, 1872, a tragedy took place. After being swindled in a railroad stock scheme, an angry mob attacked a train thought to be carrying the perpetrators. They killed the county attorney, the judge of the county court and one other man. Forty one men were charged with the crime but there were no convictions.

Judge Isaac Parker

Another lawman with a questionable reputation was Isaac Parker. On March 19, 1875, this former Missouri Representative was appointed to a position as judge in what came to be known as "The Court of the Damned." Parker became famous in the old west as "The Hanging Judge."

Baldknobbers, "Honest Men" and Law and Order Leagues

Crime was rampant and criminals seemed out of control following the War Between the States. In order to fight the crime, well-meaning men formed various secret societies to take the law into their own hands. It's often the case with vigilante groups that good intentions go bad pretty quickly.

One such group was called the "Regulators" or the "Honest Men's League" of Greene County. On May 23, 1866, these Regulators killed their first victim on this day hoping to send a message to criminals and therefore to restore order. Over in Walnut Grove on June 16, 1866, the Regulators or "Honest Men's League" of Walnut Grove proclaimed that anyone who bailed accused criminals out of jail was subject to action by the vigilantes. The Law and Order League Club was formed in St. Louis to prevent crime and immorality on October 22, 1883. On August 15, 1912, n Texas County, a "Law and Order League" was organized to investigate the illegal sale of intoxicants. (A.K.A. vigilantes chasing moonshiners).

The most famous (infamous) group formed in far southern Missouri and had the practice of meeting on treeless hills called "bald knobs." This allowed them to see the approach of anyone who might be opposed to their secret meetings. Trying to do good originally, they soon became a tyrannical group of domestic terrorists. On August 20, 1888, with the death of their leader, Nat Kinney, the Baldknobbers were finally being suppressed.

Three other leaders of the Baldnobbers were hanged on May 10, 1889 in Forsyth. The rope broke on one and he was taken back onto the scaffold and re-hanged. And, yes, these vigilantes-gone-wild were the ones described in _The Shepherd of the Hills._

Baldknobbers with horned masks waiting in ambush.

Kansas

When considering dastardly deeds, one must always think of Kansas. On January 21, 1879, the Kansas Senate approved a plan to move their border eastward thus stealing Kansas City, St. Joseph, Joplin, Weston, etc. from Missouri. This was blocked by the Missouri Legislature.

The Marsden Gang

In April of 1883, the infamous Marsden Gang of hog thieves had been bringing home the bacon but was now on the run in the Hillsboro area. One member squealed on the others to get leniency and a mob of 25-30 armed men were closing in on those still at large. They were all rooted out and captured and their careers as purloiners of porkers came to an abrupt end.

Walter Maxwell

On April 5, 1885, an Englishman in St. Louis, Walter Maxwell, murdered his wealthy friend and put the body in a trunk. St. Louis police spent $400 for a telegram to New Zealand where Maxwell was hiding. The national press followed Maxwell's 69-day trip back to Missouri with great interest. Later writers compared the events to the O.J. Simpson chase and trial.

On June 23, 1887, newspapers were reporting that "Maxwell the Chloroformer" and his friend, Preller were "doomed to die" on August 12. His mother came from England to issue an emotional plea to spare her "little cloroformer" as she called him. Then, in a surprise move, he was hanged in St. Louis on August 10 – two days earlier than scheduled.

Dr. Arthur Duestrow

On Valentine's Day, 1894, Dr. Arthur Duestrow drove his sleigh home from a three-day affair with a prostitute and shot his wife and infant son. He later explained that he wasn't Dr. Duestrow at all but Count Van Brandenburg. He also claimed at another time to be a Cardinal of the Catholic Church. The jury did not believe him to be insane. However, he was hanged at Union, MO courthouse.

George and William Taylor

On May 11, 1894, the Taylor brothers committed the horrific Meeks Family Murder of Linn County. This subject of songs and ballads saw the Meeks family axed to death then buried in a farm field. One severely-injured six-year-old (Nellie Meeks) survived to identify her attackers. Murdered that night were little Nellie's father, mother, 4-year-old sister and 18 month-old sister. An unborn fetus also died with her mother.

Nellie awoke and crawled from her shallow grave to tell the neighbors what had happened. A long chase and a dramatic trial followed. In the end, William was hanged but George managed to escape and was never found.

Harris & Dooley Clans

These people weren't like the other outlaws mentioned. They were violent but mostly just toward each other. On August 4, 1900, a jealous husband shot his wife's lover at a Doe Run, MO picnic and started a feud between the Harris and Dooley clans. That first day, several people were killed including one 16-year-old girl who was just a bystander.

After the feud in the Mineral Area one of the Harrises told his doctor, "All right, Doc – if I die, I'll be a good mineral prospect – lead in three places." Finally, after nine years the feud ended because all of the Harris and Dooley clansmen were dead.

Ma Barker

Arizona Clark was born on August 8, 1873 in Ash Grove, MO. In later life she was known by her matronly married name, Ma Barker. She was the queen bee of a notorious swarm of outlaws across southwest Missouri and other states

The Missouri Kid

On December 27, 1902, "The Missouri Kid" Rudolph and "Black Frank" Collins killed a Pinkerton Agent and made off with $14,000 from the bank at Union, MO. Justice was swift in those days and by May 8, 1904 he had been tried and was hanged.

The Missouri Kid

Francis Tumblety

Never heard of Francis Tublety? Have you heard of Jack the Ripper? Jack the Ripper did terrible things to the women on the streets of London and then the crime wave mysteriously stopped. It was just at that time that Francis Tumblety sailed for America and settled in St. Louis. A crime wave began in St. Louis with the victims being the women of the street in that city.

The strange man who dressed in military-style uniforms and made claims to be all sorts of important people died in St. Louis on May 28, 1903 and the crimes against women suddenly ended. In his home some terrible evidence was soon found including body parts and other disgusting things. He will not be missed.

Francis Tumblety

Edward Sinclair

Edward Sinclair was jailed in Springfield on January 25, 1911. His crime was small but interesting. You see, he was charged with counterfeiting nickels. Why would he bother?

Gypsies

On March 22, 1913, horses were reported missing in Jefferson County. A band of Gypsies camped there said that some of their horses seemed to be missing also. Of course they were! Traveling Gypsies have been in all sorts of trouble across the state for many decades but usually the troubles involved small-scale scams and petit thefts. In 2013 however, it was announced that a Gypsy band was being investigated for stealing children from Cape Girardeau and other towns.

The King of one Gypsy band was camped outside of Rolla when he died. His people buried him in the Rolla City Cemetery and eventually his wife and others were buried nearby. The Gypsy graves today are a tourist attraction and many stories are attached to those graves.

Quail Hunter Kennedy

Back in 1899, Quail Hunter Kennedy engineered a train robbery near Macomb, was caught, and prosecuted. Then he set himself up in the motion picture business showing movies about himself and trying to make a living as a bad example for youth.

Robert Camden

Probably a person's view of Robert Camden depended on what kind of contact you had with him. Some called him the "Robin Hood of Reynolds County" and others called him the "Scourge of the Ozarks." On May 27, 1936, he was brought from the state pen into Centerville to testify at a trial. Six pretty young women were waiting and each gave him a warm kiss. He was certainly popular with them.

While hiding from the law Camden didn't want armed men in the woods so he left notes stating that hunters in his part of the Ozarks would be shot on sight. Fishing became very popular that year! He also promised that he would do the hunting and that no one would lack for meat on their tables so he kept them supplied with venison and turkey. So, before he was captured, a family might be sitting in their home and hear a knock at the door. They would look outside and find a turkey or a quarter of venison waiting for them. This is what made him so popular with the locals.

Bertha Gifford

People will always tell you that serial killers are young or middle-aged single men. But the worst serial killer in our state's history was a woman named Bertha Gifford. She is believed to have killed seventeen men, women, and even children in Franklin and Jefferson Counties. The outrageous thing about Gifford is that she was known as a wonderful cook and a most caring person. Neighbors called her the Good Samaritan.

On August 25, 1928, Gifford was arrested while shopping in Eureka, MO. It's interesting to note that this woman who poisoned her victims with arsenic in the meals she prepared, went off to prison where she spent the rest of her life cooking for the other inmates.

Bonnie and Clyde

Bonnie Parker and Clyde Barrow were two of the most famous outlaws in American history but they were not from Missouri. However they enjoyed spending a little free time here. But when your life is all about stealing and killing, the law officers are never far away. On April 1, 1933, they were hiding in a two-story stone bungalow in Joplin. On the 13th the police moved in and one of their most famous running gun battles erupted. Somehow they escaped but two police officers were dead.

On July 20 of that same year, Bonnie and Clyde were involved in another shootout in Missouri. This time it was at the Red Crown Tavern and Tourist Court in Platte City. Somehow they escaped but were later caught by another posse in Iowa. This shootout was depicted in the 1967 movie, *Bonnie and Clyde*, but the movie depiction showed a motel sign that read, "Platte City, Iowa."

Pretty Boy Floyd

Charles Arthur Floyd was a small-time hood as a teenager stealing coins from the post office and committing other kinds of theft. Then on September 16, 1925, he committed a payroll robbery in St. Louis. He served 3 ½ years and then returned to his life of crime. On June 17, 1933, Pretty Boy Floyd and his buddies killed four policemen and their prisoner in front of the Union Station in Kansas City. This event has come to be known as the Kansas City Massacre. He later sent a note from Springfield claiming that he didn't do the evil deed in K.C.

Southwest Bank Robbery

This robbery of the famous bank in St. Louis was actually carried out by some little-known gangsters from Chicago on April 24, 1953. It's interesting because, just like an action movie, about 100 police officers were shooting it out with the gangsters. Customers and employees who were at the Southwest Bank in St. Louis that day gave details and played bit parts in a movie re-enactment later staring former Missourian, Steve McQueen.

Bob Berdella

This accomplished chef and less-than-prosperous businessman from Kansas City was born on January 31, 1949. He owned and, during the day, operated Bob's Bizarre Bazaar. At night he tortured and killed young men. He would sometimes tell his drinking buddies about the young prisoners at his home but no one believed the strange stories. Finally one young man escaped and, wearing nothing but a dog collar, ran for safety and Bob's bizarre crime spree ended.

James Earl Ray

On April 23, 1967, James Earl Ray hid in a bread bin aboard a bakery truck and escaped from Missouri's State Penitentiary. Eleven months later he was arrested for assassinating Dr. Martin Luther King, Jr. In fairness, it should be noted that many people claim that Ray did not shoot Dr. King. Even Dr. King's family think Ray may not have done the job or, at least didn't act alone.

The Pardue Brothers

On April 8, 1971, John Pardue was killed while attempting to escape from authorities in Connecticut. Earlier he and his brother, James, had bombed the Franklin County Courthouse in Union, MO as a diversion while they robbed the United Bank of Union. The Sherrif's Office and Courts were all in the Courthouse so every available policeman, deputy, and fire fighter rushed to the scene. While the first responders were busy, the Pardue Brothers entered the bank and announced their holdup.

The trouble was that the bank was only a block away from the courthouse and every law enforcement officer in the area. Somehow, the Pardues escaped. Before they were finished they had robbed five banks and killed their father and grandmother.

Martin McNally

On June 23, 1972, Martin McNally hijacked a plane at St. Louis demanding $500,000 as a ransom for the plane and crew. He got it and the plane took off. Three days later, farmers near Peru, Indiana found a submachine gun and $500,000 in cash. Then on June 29, McNally was arrested and charged with hijacking that airliner in St. Louis. When he jumped from the jet plane in flight over Peru, Indiana, the shock of the air caused him to drop his machine gun and all of the $500,000 in cash. Don't let people tell you that criminals are smart!

Ken McElroy

The entire town of Skidmore and the surrounding county of Nodaway were suffering at the hands of a terrible bully named Ken McElroy. He abused men and women and was charged with crimes 21 times. Finally, on July 10, 1981 things got so bad that the entire town assembled to discuss what they might do. While they met, McElroy drove into town and went to a nearby tavern.

The sheriff advised the people not to do anything other than form a neighborhood watch committee. Then he got in his police cruiser and left town "on business." The armed crowd went to confront McElroy and he came out of the tavern with a belligerent attitude. Several shots rang out and McElroy was hit with fire from at least two kinds of guns. The amazing thing is that 46 people were present and standing nearby but not one of them saw anything! McElroy died and no one has ever been charged.

Ray and Faye Copeland

On August 20, 1989, a tip lead officials to the Mooresville farm of Ray and Faye Copeland, a geriatric couple who were later convicted of murdering five vagrants but it seems that they probably murdered twelve or more. No one knows why – they just seemed to like killing men that no one would miss.

Lisa Montgomery

In tiny Skidmore, Missouri on December 16, 2004 a Kansas resident, Lisa Montgomery, strangled 23-year-old Bobbie Jo Stinnett then cut Bobbie Jo's unborn baby from her womb. Montgomery was caught 23 hours later in Kansas. The baby was safe but Montgomery set a new standard for inhuman behavior.

Fast Eddie

Edward Maher had been living quietly in Ozark, Missouri and, in spite of some strange stories from his family members, no one suspected who he was. Then he hit some financial hard times and he broke his cover. It turned out that he was wanted in England for a $1.5 million armored car robbery in London. He was arrested on February 8, 2012. Of course, one has to wonder, how did he spend all that money in addition to the salary that he and his wife earned from their jobs in Missouri?

Joseph Paul Franklin

This man (real name = James Clayton Vaughn) was a serial killer murdering people throughout the eastern U.S. His killings usually were prompted by the victim's race, religion, or the race of the victim's family or associates. The exact number of his killings is unknown but he was convicted of seven before being executed. The true number of victims is thought to be as high as 22.

While serving time in the prison at Potosi (Mineral Point) he groomed himself to look like Adolph Hitler. He was finally put to death by lethal injection at the Bonne Terre Correctional Center on November 20, 2013.

Missouri's Worst . . .
(Disasters)

Not So Much

Before we get into the terrible disasters, let us remember two interesting ones that could have been worse. On October 24, 1844 a tornado struck the cabin of Kansas City pioneer, John Calvin McCoy. It picked up his three-month-old son, bed and all, and carried him out of his house. He was later found, still in his bed, and safe.

Then in 1936, a strange thing happened to Hazeldell School in Laclede County. A tornado picked up the log school and moved it to another nearby location but little damage was done. Students were back at work in the school within a very short time!

New Madrid Earthquake

The largest earthquake ever to shake North America began on December 16, 1811. It was centered on the New Madrid Fault in Missouri. Often thought of as one quake, it was actually a series of many large quakes and hundreds of small ones over a period of many days. Lakes were instantly drained as other new ones were created. The Mighty Mississippi actually flowed backwards for a time. Steeples swayed and church bells rang as far away as the east coast. Luckily for Missourians, most homes and other buildings in that day were made of logs and could sway with the shaking. There were no tall buildings in 1811.

People continue to worry about that fault and about repeat quakes. Television documentaries and university research still focus on the possibilities and the state of preparedness of Missouri and nearby states. On December 3, 1990, schools and businesses closed while families stocked up on supplies. This date was predicted to see a gigantic earthquake along the New Madrid Fault. Nothing happened.

The Editor

The *Editor*, a tramp steamboat blew up at the mouth of the Missouri River killing about 100 people on July 3, 1842. Most of them were among the earliest German immigrants into the center of the state.

The Great Flood of '44

The worst flood in St. Louis history happened in June of 1844. It began to recede on June 28 but enormous destruction had been done. At its height St. Louis was flooded as far west as Broadway Avenue. East St. Louis was covered by floodwater 20 feet deep.

The Great St. Louis Fire

On May 1, 1849, the steamboat Highlander burned at the levee in St. Louis. Some folks warned that this type of fire might someday spread to the crowded wooden buildings in downtown St. Louis. Such a thing would be a disaster – and sixteen days later it was. On May 17, 1849, the Great St. Louis Fire began on the Steamboat White Cloud and spread to 22 others. It quickly spread into the city and most of the old French section of St. Louis was destroyed. Fire Captain Thomas Targee was killed fighting the fire.

Then on May 22, 1849, just five days after the great fire, business leaders in St. Louis had already decided to clear the debris, straighten the streets, widen the streets, lay new water and sewer pipes, and replace the burned wooden buildings with brick buildings. St. Louis made the decision to become an American-style city that afternoon.

The Great Cholera Epidemic

Gold was discovered at Sutter's Mill in California in 1848 but, by the time word arrived in the east, it was too late for travelers to go west because of the fearsome winters on the Great Plains and in the Rocky Mountains. Many tens of thousands of prospectors came to St. Louis and waited through the winter for a chance to ride west by horse or by steamboat. Then on December 28, 1848 the steamboat *Amaranth* arrived in St. Louis carrying cholera. The little town of St. Louis didn't have a good enough sewer system for such a large population and an epidemic of cholera broke out.

On January 5, 1849, the very first cases were reported in what would be the Great Cholera Epidemic. No one knew in those days what caused cholera so it was a fearsome and frightful occurrence. All through this month of June cholera victims were dying. Over 4000 died in St. Louis but many more died up and down the Missouri River Valley. By July 3, officials were reporting about 700 deaths per week. . On July 28, 1849, the Committee of Health declared the great cholera epidemic was over. At least 8,423 people died in St. Louis but countless others died along the Missouri River Valley to the west. The official's optimism was unfounded and people continued to die in St. Louis and to the west.

The death toll in St. Louis was running at 640 per week due to the cholera epidemic on August 3, 1849, when President Zachary Taylor declared this day to be a National Day of Fasting and Prayer. Suddenly the death toll dropped and the worst was over but one out of every ten residents had died and many more who were just there temporarily.

The Saluda

On April 9, 1852, the steamboat *Saluda* exploded at Lexington killing more than 150 people. The captain had been fighting the current at that bend for several days when he finally determined to get around or "blow the boat to hell."

The Glencoe

The passenger steamer, *Glencoe*, was moored at St. Louis boarding passengers when all three boilers exploded on April 13, 1852. The Glencoe was blown out into the river and floated downstream burning with many frantic people still on board. Some bodies were blown onto neighboring boats and shrapnel from the blast killed at least one woman in her St. Louis home.

Guns and Hoses

Rivalries between volunteer fire companies in St. Louis came to a head on May 21, 1853 as two companies engaged in a shootout. One died and nine were injured.

The Greatest Railroad Disaster

November 1, 1855 was a cold rainy day but spirits were high in the first railroad train between St. Louis and Jefferson City. At least they were until it fell through a bridge over the rain-swollen Gasconade River. On board were the mayor and entire city council of St. Louis, two military bands, dignitaries from eastern Missouri, and presidents of various railroads. A rescue train fell into the Boeuf Creek when a second bridge collapsed. 34 killed. Over 100 injured. Survivors were rescued by steamboat and taken to Hermann and Washington. The state declared November 5 to be a day of prayer and fasting to honor the victims of the Gasconade River train disaster.

The St. Louis Massacre:

The madman, Captain Nathanial Lyon arrived at the U.S. Arsenal at St. Louis on February 6, 1861. On March 13 the strange Lyon took command of the St. Louis Arsenal and Jefferson Barracks. It was the first in a series of events which saw him drag Missouri into the War Between the States.

Lyon had already presided over a massacre that happened when he led his troops against a tribe of Indians in California. California law allowed Indians to be taken as slaves and some ranchers took the women as sex slaves. One chief rescued his wife and the rancher was killed. Lyon retaliated and killed an entire tribe – the wrong tribe.

When southern sympathizers held a protest rally west of the downtown area (where St. Louis University is today), Lyon decided to spy on them. He dressed as an old woman and, bushy beard and all, walked among the crowd. Finally he decided that the group must be punished and humiliated for the act of dissent.

On May 10, 1861, Lyon ordered his troops to take the protesters as prisoners and make examples of them. They were paraded through the streets and humiliated. People began to throw stones at the soldiers and the army shot back. Ninety civilians were shot and twenty-eight died. Also shot at by union troops were William Tecumseh Sherman and Ulysses S. Grant. More violence and more deaths followed the next day.

The St. Louis Massacre: (Continued)

On May 12, 1861, a peace conference was called in St. Louis following the two-day massacre. Missouri had voted to remain neutral during the War Between the States but General Lyon refused to cooperate and threatened to "...see every man, woman, and child in the state dead and buried." Missouri was dragged into the war by Nathaniel Lyon. Lyon was probably more responsible than anyone else for the 1106 battles and skirmishes that followed on Missouri soil.

The Raid on Osceola

On September 23, 1861, Jayhawks crossed the border and sacked Osceola. The town of 3,000 people was plundered and burned to the ground, and nine local citizens were executed. When the Bushwackers did a retribution raid on Lawrence, Kansas, home of the Jayhawks, the Bushwhackers were said to be yelling, "Remember Osceola!" The raid on Osceola was later portrayed in the Clint Eastwood movie, *The Outlaw Josie Wales.*

Collapse of the Union Jail

A makeshift prison (called the Union Jail) holding women related to Quantrill's Raiders collapsed killing or injuring all of them on August 13, 1863. The building being used as a jail was actually a home owned by the famous artist, George Caleb Bingham. It had been his mother's home and was in good condition. After the tragedy, the building was examined and it looked to many as if supporting structures in the basement had been sabotaged by Union soldiers.

Eight days later Quantrill's Raiders sacked Lawrence, KS in response to the injuries and deaths of the Raiders' mothers, wives, and sisters at the Union Jail and the burning of Osceola, MO. Union General Thomas Ewing responded to the raid on Lawrence by ordering people from their homes and farms in Bass, Cass, Jackson, and part of Vernon Counties. Then his men burned and looted that area of Missouri which today is known as "The Burnt District." See George Caleb Bingham's painting, "Order No. 11" for details. Bingham was on the scene and watched it all happen.

The Sultana

The Nation's worst maritime disaster happened on the Mississippi south of Cape Girardeau on April 27, 1864. Prisoners from Andersonville and soldiers returning to Jefferson Barracks in St. Louis for discharge were on board the steamboat Sultana when it blew up. About 1,800 died that night.

The Sultana the day before she exploded with more than six times the number of allowed passengers on board.

Even though this was America's worst maritime disaster, most people don't know about it. The reason? At the time this happened the entire nation was absorbed in the news of Lincoln's assassination and the hunt for conspirators. The newspapers paid little attention to Sultana's explosion and sinking.

The Stella Blanch

Near Ste. Genevieve, the riverboat Stella Blanch exploded on October 29, 1869. One hundred and twenty-five lives were lost. In an odd development, thousands of dollars were found floating in the water afterwards.

Tornado of 1872

Shoppers scrambled for safety and three steamboats were sunk when a tornado struck St. Louis on March 30, 1872.

The St. Charles Bridge

On November 11, 1870, a railroad bridge being built across the Missouri at St. Charles collapsed killing nineteen and injuring many more. This was the first of many disasters involving that bridge. On November 8, 1879, a railroad bridge crossing the Missouri at St. Charles collapsed for the second time. Grain and livestock were thrown into the water and five men were killed.

Then on December 8, 1881, the railroad bridge collapsed for the third time! Thirty one freight cars plunged into the river. It was also proving to be a hazard for steamboats. On June 25, 1935 a Wabash railway train struck a pier on the highway bridge at St. Charles. One span crashed down onto Main Street and the train crashed into the side of a hotel. No one was hurt! However, the bridge was unusable and ferry boats were put into service.

On the first of June, 1890, the folks tried another option. This day saw the opening of the first Missouri River bridge for pedestrians, wagons, and livestock. It was a pontoon bridge that actually floated on the river at St. Charles. The winter's ice floating downstream destroyed it five months later.

Courthouse Burnings

On the subject of repeated disasters, consider Wright County's Courthouse. In 1849, the Courthouse was burned. Well, bad things sometimes happen. However, it burned again in 1862. Then Civil War soldiers burned the new Courthouse in 1863. They moved into a temporary Courthouse but it burned in 1864. Then in 1888, a terrible tornado came through Hartville and, you guessed it – there went the Courthouse. At least it wasn't another fire. Would you believe that in 1896 they had another fire at the Courthouse? Well, it happened. But in 1897 it happened again!

The Wright County Courthouse was destroyed seven times! Some courthouses in other Missouri counties burned several times but not that many times. There were many reasons why courthouses would burn. As with the Wright County buildings, some military soldiers would set fire to the courthouse as punishment to those in a place where they thought the enemy lived. It was a way to punish the local people. And, of course, there are natural and accidental fires. In America's early days it also used to be fairly common for lawyers and people being sued to set fires and destroy records which could be harmful to them in a trial. Without the records, you couldn't be convicted.

The Day Marshfield Blew Away

Known by old timers as "the day that Marshfield blew away," an F-4 tornado struck Marshfield and killed 99 on April 18, 1880. 100 more were injured. The towns of McDowell, Ozark, Linden, and Fordland were devastated. Seven died in Springfield. Fierce tornados blew through Barry, Miller, Morgan, Moniteau, and Callaway Counties also.

The Rolla Fireworks Fire

Boys playing with leftover fireworks started a fire which destroyed nineteen buildings in Rolla on July 9, 1881. There was a total of $35,000 in damages. (Nineteen buildings and only $35,000 in damages!)

The Wet Blizzard

The "wet blizzard" in Camden County saw incredible amounts of rain swell the Osage, Glaize, and Niangua Rivers causing great loss life and property on February 20, 1882.

Epic Elevator Failure

Shakespeare wrote, "Beware the Ides of March." A freight elevator loaded with sheet metal fell on factory workers in St. Louis killing five and injuring more on March 15, 1882.

Sportsman's Park

A fireworks factory exploded on the grounds of Sportsman's Park in St. Louis on December 30, 1882. Neighbors and baseball fans had complained for years that it wasn't good to have an explosives factory next to a stadium.

On April 16, 1898, the St. Louis Browns were playing the Chicago Cubs when a fire broke out in Sportsman's Park. 40 people were hurt in the panic. The lawsuits forced the team into bankruptcy.

Town of Brotherton Disappears

A raging Missouri River eroded away the land which held the booming town of Brotherton, Missouri and it was swallowed on June 20, 1882. Not a trace remains.

The Webb City Miners

February 13, 1886 was a bad day in Webb City. Two miners in were tamping 18 sticks of dynamite into place when the sticks exploded. A single foot was the largest human remain found.

Jackson County Tornado

On May 11, 1886, a tornado hit the Missouri River Railroad Bridge then took the top off the Jackson County Courthouse. Fifteen children were killed inside the Lathrop School and ten others around the area. Many of the county's records were destroyed or lost.

Mysterious House Explosion

A newspaper in St. Louis reported on November 1, 1887 that a house mysteriously exploded in St. Louis and, "Nearly a dozen persons were hurled without warning into eternity." Others were injured.

Union Station Circus Train Wreck

On November 3, 1887, a circus train wrecked in Union Station at St. Louis. Lions, a tiger, hyenas, ibexes, and more escaped into the station. A boa constrictor was cut up by the train's wheels. Some "bad boys" were throwing rocks at the animals. A few monkeys got away and so did the "bad boys."

The Mill Creek Explosion

On July 26, 1892, the newspaper headlines said, "Houses Demolished—Railroad Tracks and Trains Swallowed Up—Several Persons Killed and Injured—Miraculous Escapes and Rescues" after the Mill Creek Sewer Explosion in St. Louis.

The Tornado of 1896

On May 27, 1896, the costliest and third deadliest tornado in U.S. history roared through the St. Louis metro area. 255 people died and over a thousand were injured. Eight days later a newspaper in Jefferson County reported, "Great as the loss of life and property has been the citizens of St. Louis [who] have bravely announced that they will provide for their own need, and do not desire any outside assistance. As they have always been among the first and most liberal in helping other stricken communities, it was natural that they should receive offers of assistance from all over the globe, but all such offers have been respectfully declined." How different from today's attitude!

One newspaper reported that three days after the terrible St. Louis tornado, 140,000 people came through Union Station in that one day. Most were curious gawkers but 83 were arrested for looting.

The Kirkwood Fire

On December 21, 1896, a terrible fire swept down the main business section of Kirkwood. The event became such a catastrophe because the town had no fire department.

The Rich Hill Mine Explosion

Twenty-four miners were killed in a coal mine explosion at Rich Hill on March 29, 1888.

The Clark County Trestle

A Santa Fe R.R. passenger train carrying 350 fell through a trestle near Medell and Revere, MO (Clark County) leaving many dead and injured on May 6, 1892.

The Missouri City Train Wreck

A terrible mail train wreck occurred at Missouri City when the train fell through a rain-weakened trestle killing seven people including five mail clerks on June 27, 1897.

The Kirksville Tornado

Three hundred buildings were destroyed and 34 people died when a tornado hit Kirksville on April 27, 1899.

K.C. Convention Hall Fire

On April 4, 1900, fire destroyed Kansas City's Convention Hall and surrounding buildings. The Democrat's National Convention was only three months away so they quickly built one of the world's largest arenas on the site. Badges were being worn all around town saying, "Kansas City Spirit."

The Mule Barn Fire

Almost 300 horses and mules were killed in a fire which swept through the stables of the St. Louis garbage contractor on November 6, 1901.

Barney Oldfield's Crash

Blinded by dust, America's first famous racecar driver, Barney Oldfield lost control of his "Green Dragon" and slammed into a fence at the Fairground Race Track in St. Louis on August 28, 1904. The car cut one spectator in half and killed another. Many more were injured. Oldfield would never race again.

The World's Fair Train Wrecks

A special train running to the World's Fair in St. Louis wrecked at Kimmswick killing and injuring many on April 30, 1904. Hurrying to the Fair, the engineer sped too fast onto a siding. Reports from that time say that eight died and one report said that fifty died.

Another passenger train loaded with people bound for the St. Louis World's Fair collided head-on with a freight train near Warrensburg on October 10 of that year. Thirty were reported dead and dozens more injured.

Missouri Pavilion Fire

A fire destroyed the Missouri Building at the World's Fair two weeks before it was to close (November 19, 1904). Most of the treasures inside were saved. The U.S. Marines rushed in to save the bell that Missourians had bought with their donations for the USS Missouri.

The Marysville Circus Tent

A Ringling Brothers Circus tent holding 15,000 people collapsed at Marysville on September 18, 1905. Two men were killed immediately, five people were seriously injured and forty others trampled.

The Luxemburg Surprise

On April 26, 1907, two volunteer firemen were killed and eight injured when a building blew up in Luxemburg (St. Louis County). The fire was set by arsonists and no one realized the building was full of dynamite.

The Windsor M-K-T Explosion

A black powder explosion at the M-K-T Railroad depot in Windsor killed 14 and severely injured at least 8 more on September 15, 1908. A "sizeable part" of the Windsor depot was destroyed also.

The Cardinals Team Train

One of the most interesting disasters in Missouri history was one in which no Missourians were hurt. On July 11, 1911, the Cardinals were on their way to Boston and their sleeping cars were in the front of the train. The engine was so noisy and the engineer was so "whistle crazy" that the team complained and their cars were moved to the rear of the train. That night the train crashed down an embankment and the front cars were all destroyed killing 14. Cardinal players helped to rescue survivors but, thanks to the late-night move, no Cardinals were hurt.

The Dentist's Cigar

A Dentist lighting his cigar set the post office ablaze in Ava on October 4, 1911. About 200 men and women managed to keep the fire from burning the hotel next door and only two buildings were lost.

The Fenton Fire

Much of downtown Fenton was destroyed by a fire on April 19, 1913. When it was over, only two churches and two other buildings remained.

The Brush Creek Train Wreck

A Frisco passenger train fell through a trestle near Lebanon killing 45 people on September 15, 1914. Most of them drowned in the rain-swollen Brush Creek.

The K.C. Stockyards Fire

On October 16, 1917, a disastrous fire raged through the Kansas City Stockyards killing 17,000 cattle and hogs. Thirty-thousand others were set free and survived. Many had to be rounded up in Downtown K.C.

The Influenza Pandemic

Missouri's first cases of Spanish Flu were reported on October 4, 1918. As the flu pandemic hit its peak on December 3, 1918, St. Louis reported 1,476 new cases on that day alone. This pandemic would eventually kill millions around the globe. In the miserable conditions of World War I more people died from influenza than from wounds.

The MO-PAC Express

Thirty seven people were killed and 138 injured when a Missouri Pacific express train slammed into the back of a local train near Sulphur Springs on August 6, 1922.

The Tri-State Tornado

The "Tri-State Tornado" struck Missouri, Illinois and Indiana on March 18, 1925. It killed 695 people and injured more than 2000. Besides being the worst tornado in the nation's history, this one behaved in some very unusual ways.

The Great Poplar Bluff Twisters

On May 9, 1927, a tornado in Poplar Bluff killed 104 and injured 350 more. In all 225 people were killed as this group of twisters swept through southern Missouri and Arkansas.

Another Fierce Tornado

Yet another deadly tornado in St. Louis killed 85, injured 1500 and destroyed much of the city from the Central West End eastward to the Mississippi. The date was September 29, 1927.

The West Plains Dance Hall

A dance hall exploded in West Plains completely destroying the building and killing 37 people on April 13, 1928. 22 others were injured in this Friday the 13th tragedy.

'30s Airline Crashes

Two airliners crashed in Missouri with interesting results. On May 6, 1935 a TWA airliner crashed in a muddy field near Atlanta, MO killing five. Then on August 5, 1936 a Chicago and Southwestern airliner crashed in fog near Lambert Field killing eight. This shows how few people used to fly on airplanes in those days.

The MSU Christmas Tower

A forty eight foot tower for Christmas decorations was built atop the Administration Building of the Southwest Missouri State University (now Missouri State University) in Springfield. On June 10, 1938 lightning stuck it and sent it falling into a classroom in an adjacent building. Several teachers in one class were injured.

Cape's Deadly Twister

A tornado destroyed over 200 homes and killed 23 in Cape Girardeau on May 21, 1949.

The State Fair Tornado

A deadly tornado struck the Missouri State Fair at Sedalia on August 2, 1952 catching many people in pavilions, tents, and out in the open.

The Katie Jane Memorial Home Fire

On February 17, 1957, a nursing home fire in Warrenton caught fire and killed 72. During the subsequent investigation, the notion of arson was dismissed as the final determination was that the blaze started from an undetermined cause. Despite this finding, the Home had been operating without a license, had inadequate fire escapes and had no sprinkler system. In addition, there was no alarm system or evacuation plan, while some residents were locked in their rooms, a common practice of that period.

The MO-Kan Tornado

On May 20, 1957, just south of Kansas City a tornado swept in from Kansas and killed 37. Over 500 were injured.

The Freemont Tornado

May 21 has been a bad date for tornadoes in Missouri. On that day in 1957 an F5 tornado hit Freemont killing 75. That same day a tornado killed eight in Desloge and Cantwell. These twisters were spawned by the same storm which created the MO-Kan Tornado less than 24 hours earlier.

The Mid-Town Tornado

During the early morning hours of February 10, 1959 a tornado went through St. Louis damaging several landmark buildings including Channel Two, The Arena, and the Ferris wheel at the Highlands Amusement Park. More than 2000 people were left homeless, almost 2000 buildings were damaged, 41 destroyed, and 21 people died.

State Fair Stock Car Catastrophe

Even though the area was restricted and closed, 50 fans climb under fence. Then a stock car at MO State Fair (Sedalia) blew a tire. Four were killed and many injured. The date was August 28, 1965

Times Beach

On the 30th of July, 1974, a mysterious toxin which had killed horses and birds around eastern Missouri was finally identified. Russell Bliss had been spraying dioxin. Hit worst of all was Times Beach. On February 23, 1983, the EPA announced the buyout of Times Beach, Missouri which Russell Bliss had sprayed with dioxin-laced waste oil. Popular bumper stickers of the day read "Ignorance is Bliss." Contaminated soil was incinerated and Time Beach is now Route 66 State Park. The park is nice but an entire community was destroyed.

Coates House Hotel Fire

The big hotel had been one of Kansas City's finest with a long list of distinguished visitors. Then it gradually fell into hard times with rooms renting for $12.00 per week. On January 28, 1978, the hotel burned and caused the worst loss of life by fire in Kansas City's history. Twenty people died in the fire. Since that day it has been rebuilt and consists of luxury apartments and condominiums.

The Hyatt Regency Collapse

A walkway around the interior of the Hyatt Regency Hotel in Kansas City collapsed on July 17, 1981 killing 114 people during a tea dance. 200 more were injured.

The K.C. Tanker Truck Explosion

On November 29, 1988, the Kansas City Fire Department responded to reports of a large truck on fire. It turned out the the tanker truck was loaded with ammonium nitrate which exploded and killed six fire fighters. The memorial service at Arrowhead Stadium saw over 5,000 fire fighters in attendance from the United States and around the world.

The St. Charles Tanker Truck Explosion

It was September 13, 1990 when a tanker hauling 8000 gallons of fuel collided with another semi and exploded on Interstate 70 east of Highway 94. Soon every vehicle on every highway in the "Westplex" area was stuck in traffic.

The Great Flood of '93

1992 had been a year of terrible flooding on Missouri's rivers. Then 1993 turned out to be even worse! On July 12, 1993, all major news networks sent their anchors to St. Louis where all national news broadcasts originated. The flood was at its peak with 24 dead so far. On the 16th the great flood was in progress when a levee broke near St. Charles. By this time the mouth of the Missouri River was 20 miles upstream from its normal location.

On the 18th the Mississippi River crested at 46.9 feet in St. Louis which was 3.7 feet higher than the previous record. Water flowed past the Gateway Arch at the rate of 7.5 million gallons per second. On July 20th everyone thought the flooding had peaked but this day saw two more inches of rain in eastern Missouri. The Mississippi climbed ever higher to 47.05 feet.

On July 30, 1993, the Monarch Levee in Chesterfield Valley gave way and the entire area was flooded. Highway 40, Spirit of St. Louis Airport and other important features were covered by the Missouri River. Dozens of propane tanks were trying to float and broke loose in South St. Louis as flood waters covered the area. People were evacuated as authorities feared propane explosions. All across central and eastern Missouri the communities and farmers dealt with unique problems caused by this "500-year-flood".

The year's flooding reached its peak on August 1. Also on this day the Burger King Riverboat Restaurant and the minesweeper, U.S.S. Inaugural were both torn from their moorings on the St. Louis levee. Flood waters carried them downstream where the minesweeper eventually sank. The Mississippi river finally dropped below flood stage on September 13 after a total of 124 days of flooding.

The Fenton Pallet Fire

A spectacular fire occurred in Fenton on August 4, 1997. More than 180,000 wooden pallets burned at a recycling plant.

State's Worst Traffic Accident

In the worst traffic accident in Missouri history, 98 cars collided on rain-slick pavement at the intersection of Highway 79 and Interstate 70 on April 15, 1998. Somehow there were no fatalities!

Taum Sauk Reservoir Collapse

The Taum Sauk Reservoir collapsed sending a fifteen-foot-tall wall of water and mud into the valley below and destroying the Johnson Shut-Ins State Park on December 14, 2005. It took years for the park to recover but the Johnson Shut-Ins are a natural playground again.

The Tornado Outbreak of '06

On the terrible day of March 11, 2006 tornados touched down in Taney, Douglas, Phelps, Reynolds, Iron, Madison, St. Francois, Ste. Genevieve, Jefferson, Monroe, and Perry Counties in Missouri. This was the beginning of a four-day "tornado outbreak sequence" which saw 105 tornados spawned (one of them an F4), thirteen deaths, and a great deal of damage in places like Kansas City. The outbreak covered most of the central United States.

The next Day tornados touched down in Jackson, Ray, Carroll, Randolph, Monroe, Ralls, Pettis, Cooper, Henry, Benton, Saline, Morgan, Howard, Audrain, Pike, Bates, Cass, Henry, Johnson, Vernon, Cedar, St. Clair, Scotland, Clark, Barton, Dade, Polk, Hickory, Newton, Lawrence, Christian, Green, Webster, Wright, Laclede, Callaway, Osage, Montgomery, Warren, Pike, and Lincoln Counties in Missouri.

The Bootheel Twisters

On April 2, 2006, a string of tornadoes ripped through the Bootheel and destroyed 60% of Caruthersville. Several churches, the airport, many homes and businesses along with the middle school and high school were destroyed. Somehow no lives were lost!

The Clinton Elks Lodge

The three-story Elks Lodge building collapsed in Clinton while about 50 members were dining on the second floor on June 26, 2006. Many were rescued but the chapter president died.

The Red Regiment Crash

A horrific wreck near Gray Summit involving busses of the St. James Red Regiment Band stacked two busses and a semi. It was August 5, 2010 when a 19-year-old man from Sullivan was buried in his pickup under the wreckage. Many were injured but somehow only two were killed. The pickup driver was "texting" as he drove I-44 and started the chain reaction crash.

The Lambert International Tornado

An F-3 tornado touched down in New Melle on April 22, 2011 and continued eastward through Bridgeton and Maryland Heights. Along the way it hit the terminal complex at Lambert International Airport head on.

The Joplin Tornado

A terrible tornado destroyed a huge portion of Joplin and left scores of citizens dead on May 22, 2011. Worst hit was the city's main hospital. Over 7,500 homes were also hit. The death toll was over 160. The storm was awesome – the community was inspiring.

Missouri's Most Extreme . . .

EXTREME COLD & SNOW:

The Mississippi was frozen over and a saloon keeper set up business in the middle of the river on January 17, 1854. His new location was so popular that he added a "ten pin alley." Soon seven additional saloons were operating in the middle of the river and away from any authorities. On January 7, 1856, the Mississippi River was frozen over again and people were walking across. St. Louis saloonkeepers were once more doing a great business in the middle of the river and out of the reach of any law.

On both nights of February 4 & 5, 1855, temperatures of 20 degrees below zero were recorded in Greene County. Snow was at a depth of 18 to 20 inches. It took the stage from Bolivar to Springfield an extra two days for that 30 mile trip.

It was still severely cold several months later. Records show a "sharp frost" in Greene County on August 19, 1855. That's correct – a bad frost in the middle of August! This was the beginning of one of the worst winters ever seen. See the preceding paragraph about the winter of 1855-56.

On January 4, 1884, temperatures across eastern Missouri dropped to more than 25 degrees below zero.

Winter stayed around all through the spring of 1890. It was March 23, 1890 when after a terrible windstorm three days earlier, twenty or more inches of snow fell at many eastern Missouri places. Then a week later (March 30, 1890) "The

Great Blizzard of '90" began. It brought over 20 inches of snow over two days to parts of Missouri.

The next day, March 31, the _Globe-Democrat_ carried a little story on page six of the daily paper commenting on the worst blizzard in the city's history. It stated, "...a spell of weather affected all lines of business and pleasure in a most disagreeable way." How does that compare with coverage of a storm today?

The coldest night in Missouri's recorded history was on February 13, 1905 when temperatures plummeted to 40° below zero at Warsaw, MO!

May frost? Frost covered the entire state the morning of May 25, 1925, as temperatures dropped into the lower 30s. Louisiana, MO, bottomed out to a chilly 26°F. But this wasn't the first time. On May 29, 1866, a heavy frost covered Springfield greatly injuring early wheat and garden vegetables. By June 1, 1866 newspapers were reporting that, due to frosts in late May, "Spring was very backward" and not half of the corn crop was planted.

January of 1940 was the coldest month for the state. Counting all of the highs and lows, the average temperature during that month was only 15.3 degrees!

Incredible cold during the years from 1976, 1977, and 1978 caused climatologists to predict that we were entering a new ice age. It snowed on January 9, 1978 in eastern Missouri and it stayed so cold that the day started the record 71 straight days with snow on the ground. That winter of 78-79 was the coldest in Missouri's history.

From December 20th to the 24th 1989 – Missouri experienced a terrible cold spell. Temperatures dipped to -20 in Columbia, and -16 in St. Louis and Farmington. Wind chills stayed below -25 degrees for 51 straight hours in Columbia! Can you say, "Frozen water pipes?"

The central part of the state received over a foot of snow and east-central Missouri got ice on December 2, 2006. St. Louis alone had over 500,000 homes and businesses without electricity.

A blizzard dumped a record snowfall on Mid-Missouri with 20 inches of snow, strong winds, and below zero wind chills. On February 1, 2011 Forty four counties were declared "disaster areas." Interstate 70 was closed all across the state.

EXTREME HEAT:

For many years, July of 1930 held the record for the hottest individual month in the state's history. But on July 31, 2012 it was announced that this month ended as the hottest July in Missouri's recorded history. There were 28 days of temps. at 90° or above, 15 of days at least 100°, and eight days over 105°. To make things worse, every single county in the state was declared a drought disaster area.

1936 and 1954 were the two hottest summers in the state's history. April 13, 1936 was a warm spring day! Thermometers in Kansas City were reading 113 degrees. On June 24, 1934, the temperature hit 110 degrees in St. Louis, the eighth day in a row for temps over 100. During the heat wave people fled their brick homes and slept in Forest Park. The death toll was 217.

By July 14, 1936, Missouri was gripped by the terrible heat wave. This one took over 400 lives in St. Louis alone. By August 14, people realized that it might be a good idea to sleep on the porch or in the park. On this day, the temperature in Kansas City was 113 degrees. Of course there was no air conditioning in 1936 and because of the Great Depression, many people didn't even have electricity or fans. Missouri was struggling through what was so far the hottest month in history in late July. Thousands of city people were sleeping in parks and along highways looking for relief from their houses and apartments.

It's hard to imagine, but things got even worse on July 14, 1954 when temperatures reached 118° in both Union, MO and Warsaw, MO. 118° still stands as the hottest in Missouri's recorded history.

Missouri was in another heat wave when on July 11, 1966 there were 146 deaths reported in St. Louis alone.

Thirty-two more heat-related deaths occurred on July 13, 1980. Area hospitals were running out of space for the bodies because of the ongoing heat wave.

EXTREME RAIN:

It was a gulley washer on June 22, 1947 when Holt, Missouri received 12 inches of rain in just 42 minutes! Of course that's a world record. Then, on July 20, 1965, over 18 inches of rain fell in 24 hours in Edgarton, MO.

On May 7, 2000, Union, Missouri received over 14 inches of rain in just 6 ½ hours. Downstream from Union the flooding killed two people on this day. Three hundred homes were severely damaged or destroyed in flooding of the Flat Creek, Bourbeuse, and Meramec Rivers. One entire mobile home park was washed away. This writer had several students in his class the next day who were suddenly homeless.

EXTREME DROUGHT:

The drought was so bad on July 2, 1901 that every single wagon in St. Peters was called into service hauling drinking water to town from the Cave Springs. That was the second driest year in the state's history with average precipitation across Missouri being less than 26 inches.

November of 1904 was the driest month in our history with only 2.22 inches of 'precip'

Of course the worst drought years were during the 1930s – the years of the Dust Bowl.

EXTREME ICE:

A rain, sleet, and snow storm prevailed from the 16 to the 19th of December, 1924. Fully three-fourths of the state was covered by a solid sheet of ice the last half of the month. For severity and duration, and resulting damage and loss it was unimaginable.

AN EXTREME SHIFT IN THE WEATHER:

It was November 11, 1911. On this 11-11-11 day, record warm temperatures were set all across Missouri. Then an incredible cold front brought a wind shift and falling temperatures. Sample temperatures across the state include Columbia that went from 82° to 13°, Hannibal fell from 82° to 16°, Kansas City dropped from 76° to 11°, Saint Louis from 78° to 18° and Springfield dropping from 80° to 13°.

Worst hit may have been the hunters who left in the morning wearing light clothing and walking miles from their homes or camps. With the early afternoon's balmy temperature came "rapidly moving dark boiling mass of clouds accompanied by lightning, thunder, rain, hail that eventually turned to sleet and snow." Many hunters lost their lives across the state on that day.

EXTREME POLLUTION:

It was reported that a "vast smoke" drifted across the Ozarks for four days beginning on July 3, 1863. It was probably from some gigantic grass fire in Kansas or the Indian Territory (Oklahoma).

The air pollution was so bad in St. Louis on February 23, 1923 that the Missouri Botanical Garden made plans to move out of town. They bought a large tract of land in Gray Summit, Missouri for that purpose. It came to be known as the Shaw Arboretum and now, as the Shaw Nature Reserve.

The following excerpt from the book *Mysterious Missouri* tells of some other views of the extreme pollution that used to exist in the Show-Me State:

Today our politicians tell us that high gasoline prices are good for us. They will force us to use more trains, subways, and busses. They don't want to think about those of us who don't have trains, subways, and busses coming to our houses. They have always done stuff like that. If they don't know how to fix a problem they will tell us that it's really a good thing or it's good for us.

For many years, St. Louis was a city with many factories and many homes all heated with coal and coal also powered the factories and trains all through the city. Black coal smoke was everywhere. People had trouble breathing. Laundry hung out to dry soon turned gray and everything was a sad and depressing dark dingy disgusting mess.

In 1870, Mayor Nathan Cole said, "The smoke will roll heavenward from her (the city's) furnaces, mill, machine shops, and factories – and shall cover like a silver sheen her hills and valleys far and near." How's that for a pretty promise? The air full of smoke and everything far and near covered with dust and soot. Thanks, Mr. Mayor.

But four years later things weren't getting any better. In November of 1906, people were heating up their homes and the air was getting thick. Schools had to be closed because of air pollution. Most places didn't have electricity yet so schools had to depend on sunlight coming in the windows for the kids to read and do their work. The smoke over the city was so bad that the sunlight was blocked out.

(Continued excerpt from the book *Mysterious Missouri* that tells of some other views of the extreme pollution that used to exist in the Show-Me State.)

In 1923, the air pollution was so bad in St. Louis that the Missouri Botanical Garden made plans to move out of town. They bought a large tract of land in Gray Summit, Missouri for that purpose. Today that's a popular place first known as the Shaw Arboretum and now, as the Shaw Nature Reserve.

A Chamber of Commerce official in St. Louis was trying to tell people that air pollution was a good thing in 1923. He said, "We can only hope that visitors will regard each piece of soot as evidence of our industry".

The next year the smoke and smog were so bad in St. Louis that cars were crashing and thieves were committing hold-ups while "broad daylight" was actually darkness. Folks on the sidewalks of St. Louis carried umbrellas because the air pollution was so bad. The soot would attract water droplets in the air and fall as large and small globs of black goo on everyone below.

In 1932, the Great Depression was going on and people were forced to burn cheap coal in their homes and businesses. This cheap coal had more sulfur and other bad stuff in it and it made the air pollution much worse. Other people burned wood which didn't make such bad smoke but it made more of it. It made the sky so dark that the street lights had to be on all day long.

Some Depression-poor people had moved into Forest Park and were digging a very low-grade coal from the ground. Then they would stay on and live in the holes. Selling the coal for pennies and living in the holes – for them life was truly the pits.

(Continued excerpt from the book *Mysterious Missouri* that tells of some other views of the extreme pollution that used to exist in the Show-Me State.)

November 28, 1939 came to be known as "Black Tuesday" in St. Louis. A cloud of thick smoke covered the downtown area. The street lights had to be turned on but traffic was still snarled and there were lots of car wrecks because, even with the street lights and headlights, drivers still couldn't see where they were going.

Do you remember when I said that politicians would rather tell us that bad things are good than to do something to actually solve the problems? They think solving problems might inconvenience the voters and they (the politicians) will lose some votes. That's why this air pollution thing went on for so many years. But finally, on February 24, 1940, a man stepped forward with a plan. Mayor Raymond Tucker presented his plan to end the air pollution problems. Many others objected but he was able to start his plan and he was extremely successful. Today one of the biggest streets in St. Louis is named for this brave problem solver.

OTHER EXTREMES:

An Extreme Storm

Many extreme storms were reported in the earlier chapter on Disasters. But this one was no disaster. On the 2nd of July, 1875, a weather service log book reported "a small shower of bullfrogs" in St. Louis. (A tornado passed through a pond or marsh?)

Extreme Personnel Problems

On January 4, 1911, the *Mountain Grove Journal* was reporting that "The manager of the telephone system at Ava is advertising for an old maid blind in one eye and without a tooth in her head to take a position as "hello" girl (telephone operator) in the Ava central office. It seems that every girl the Ava central office employs gets married as soon as she learns the work of the office."

Extreme Lightning

Five people were killed by lightning in one day in St. Louis County. On May 29, 1974, four were freshman girls at JFK High School in Manchester.

Extreme Hail

A hail storm with baseball-sized stones hit Lambert Airport, Hazelwood and Florissant on April 10, 2001. Every roof in those areas was damaged along with more than 60,000 cars and several aircraft.

Extreme Resourcefulness

How do you keep warm in a blizzard? Well, we found out when on January 30-31, a blizzard struck areas from the Ozarks up through the St. Louis suburbs. Nurses at St. John's Mercy in Town & Country, Missouri noticed a marked increase in births nine months after the blizzard.

Missouri's Biggest Mistakes . . .

Getting Along with Neighbors

On August 6, 1838, Mormons and "Gentiles" fought at Gallatin, MO. Following the expulsion of the Mormons from Jackson County, this "battle" saw twenty-two deaths and the expulsion from the state of 10,000 Mormons. Mormon wars followed in Illinois and Utah. While it is true that the Mormons were mistreated, it is also true that they had a terrible record of getting along with other families who lived nearby. Thankfully, that is all different today!

"Exterminating" People

People are not cockroaches and are not to be killed en masse but on October 27, 1838 – Governor Boggs issued the "Extermination Order" declaring that, "The Mormons must be treated as enemies, and must be exterminated or eliminated from the state..." The next day a group of Mormons at Shoal Creek (Haughn's Mill) met to ready themselves against attack.

A Failure to Communicate

The Mormons mentioned just above had been instructed by Joseph Smith to leave the place and move to Far West but the community's leader didn't share the instructions. They had two days to live. Why didn't the leaders tell the others what Joseph Smith had said? Two days after that the Haughn Well in Caldwell County was filled with Mormon bodies after an attack by a mob or militia from surrounding counties.

Failure to Finish Things

On June 25, 1976, Governor Bond realized that no one had ever revoked Governor Boggs' Extermination Order so, on this day, Bond repealed the order and, after 138 years, it was no longer legal to kill Mormons in Missouri.

Slavery

Nothing could be more wrong than making slaves of other human beings. So on August 30, 1861, General John C. Fremont proclaimed that all slaves owned by southern sympathizers were now free.

Slavery

Abraham Lincoln quickly revoked the proclamation of Fremont and declared that the slaves were still slaves. Fremont called Lincoln was "an imbecile" and Lincoln retaliated against Fremont.

Look Before You Shoot!

On July 15, 1869 the *Missouri Weekly Patriot* in Springfield reported that Mat Harbert of Cassville sent his wife and children to the loft because a grizzly bear was in the wheat field. He shot the monster and then moved in for a closer look where he found it had been his family's mule in the wheat field.

Stop Forest Park!

A mass meeting called for the resignation of state lawmakers who favored the purchase of Forest Park. At the May 4, 1876 meeting, opponents said that the park was too far from the city to be of any use and that it was just a playground for the rich. Of course Forest Park in St. Louis is a wonderful place full of free things for both the rich and the poor. It was also an important part of the city's ability to host the 1904 World's Fair.

We Want Nothing to Do with Them!

It was a sad day on August 22, 1876 when St. Louis City and County separated and became politically independent from each other. It has hurt both of them over the many years. The actual legal separation took place on July 18, 1878.

Go Ahead and Shoot.

On March 8, 1877, the *Neosho Times* reported that in Washburn, MO a show was in progress in which one performer asked people to shoot at him with a rifle. He would then catch the bullet with a stick. Instead, he caught it with the side of his head. Oops!

Poor Mark Twain.

People must have felt sorry for Mark Twain on December 20, 1877 when the *Post-Dispatch* reported that Mark Twain's books were no longer selling well. His latest book, *Tom Sawyer*, was singled out as being a disappointment. We can always count on the *Post-Dispatch* for accuracy.

Who's Driving that Thing?

The steamboat *Joseph Kinney* ran into the Booneville Bridge then, after repairs, ran into the Kansas City Bridge. After more repairs, she ran into the Glasgow Bridge on April 13, 1882 and was destroyed.

Deciding to be Beautiful

Who's the fairest of them all? On November 20, 1885 in St. Louis it was the beautiful socialite, Kate Brewington Bennett. This toast of society was envied for her lily-white complexion. They didn't know that she had been taking small amounts of arsenic to keep herself pale. She didn't know that it was a poison if it accumulated in your system. She is buried in Bellefontaine Cemetery.

Don't Play with Dynamite!

At Nevada, MO on November 21, 1886 three boys loaded a stump with powder and attached a fuse to it. Retiring to a safe distance they awaited the explosion until they thought the fuse had gone out. They went to the stump to ascertain the cause of failure. Just as they reached it an explosion occurred, and they were all seriously injured.

Don't Stop on the Tracks!

On September 30, 1888, Peter Guthrell of Pevely was thrown from his buggy when his frightened horse ran wild. Joseph Govereau managed to stop the horse and catch it – right on the railroad tracks. It was a big mistake and his last!

Don't Feed the Bears.

A big show was playing in Maxville on May 5, 1890 and this was followed up by a traveling company of bears, goats and a big monkey. One man said the keeper put his hand into the bear's mouth, so he concluded he could do the same. Sad mistake. Don't try this at home!

What Were They Thinking?

The first Missouri River Bridge (other than a rail bridge) was opened on June 1, 1890. It was a pontoon bridge that actually floated on the river at St. Charles. The winter's ice floating downstream destroyed it five months later. They had to know that winter's ice would come!

Don't Drink The Water!

Another bad mistake was a series of decisions in which the city fathers of St. Louis tried to tell everyone that the nasty water coming from their taps and drinking fountains was just fine. Back as early as May 6, 1888, St. Louis residents were finding eels in their sinks. The water commissioner said that eels and minnows could easily pass through the filters when they were young and then would grow while they lived in the settling basins. But don't worry – he claimed that they don't harm the water but actually make it better.

Don't Drink The Water! (Continued)

By 1895, better filters had been installed so there were no more eels and minnows coming from people's water taps. Now it was miniature crabs. On May 9 the Health Commissioner said that seeing them was actually a good thing. The water used to be so muddy that people couldn't see critters but now it was clear enough that they were clearly visible.

In 1902, St. Louis leaders were still concerned about their water supply. On March 10 one said, "We have reached the time of year when our water turns from the milky gray of winter to a warm chocolate color." But they knew that neither milky gray or warm chocolate would be good enough for the visitors who would soon be arriving from all over for the World's Fair. They found good water (as sweet and clean as heaven's nectar) in the upper Meramec near Sullivan on March 10 but could think of no way to transport enough of it to supply St. Louis.

On March 19, 1903, a trace element showed up in the St. Louis drinking water. It had earlier been put into a sewage canal in Chicago. This completely destroyed Chicago's claim that their pollution could not affect St. Louis. It was coming right down the Illinois River and into the drinking water of places like Peoria, St. Louis, and Cape Girardeau.

Finally on March 21, 1904, St. Louis got its new water purification system just barely in time for the World's Fair. Now at least the city's water no longer had "body".

This Is Really Powerful!

There used to be a military museum on South Broadway in St. Louis. But on April 22, 1900, a tour guide was showing visitors an artillery shell from the Spanish American war and explaining how powerful it was when he accidentally dropped it. No more museum!

Them Pesky Horseless Carriages!

A car in St. Louis burst into flames while driving down Grand Avenue. On April 27 1901, the _Globe_ commented, "This destroys what little confidence we had begun to repose in autos. A horse may run away, but he can't burn up. An automobile may do both."

Them Wonderful Horseless Carriages!

On May 18, 1902, the _Globe-Democrat_ was reporting that the automobile was going to result in "a more perfect state of public health." Compared to horses, maybe, but what would today's environmentalists say about the automobile being good for our health?

Let the Cubs Have Him.

On December 12. 1903, the Cardinals traded away "Three Fingers Brown" to the Cubs thinking that his handicap would keep him from a full career. He went on to win 230 more games for the Cubs and lead them to four league championships. Big mistake!

Buy Your License Here!

The wisdom of a Missouri judge revealed itself on June 1, 1905. He ruled that auto license plates in Missouri were valid only for the jurisdiction where they were purchased. Therefore, motorists must purchase a new license for each and every county they passed through.

Here – Take My Seat.

In order to seat more patrons (in the orchestra pit), on December 8, 1906 the Garrick Theater in St. Louis put the orchestra on a rigged "bridge" behind the stage. The platform collapsed dropping the musicians and timbers onto actors and stage hands below. That music sounds a little flat!

Wait 'Til We Come to a Complete Stop.

On February 24, 1908, a deputy U.S. Marshal tried to get off a moving elevator at the American Bank in St. Louis. He got trapped between the elevator car and the next floor. Of course his injuries were fatal.

Never Put It in Writing.

Miss Lucy Maupin of Valley Park got tired of waiting. Engaged for seventeen years, she had enough and sued Richard Marsden of Hillsboro for $15,000. Marsden said he never proposed to her and that he had married someone else last month. However, Miss Maupin said he proposed on June 4, 1892 and she had been saving Richard's letters. She presented them to a court on July 24, 1909. Oh my!

Chivalry Is Not Dead. (But the Ladies Are.)

It was on May 11, 1910 that the steamboat, *City of Saltillo* punctured its hull on a rock near Glen Park, MO, women and children were allowed off the sinking boat first. However, the boat hadn't yet reached the shore and the ladies were crowded off the gangplank into the Mississippi. Five women and a baby died but the gallant men were all OK.

Singing Hymns? Disgraceful!

Fines of $36 were charged to some boys from Golden City who were charged with singing sacred songs out on the public street back on April 18, 1912.

Then on June 27 of that same year, several young men were arrested at Liberal for singing "Nearer My God to Thee." You may remember that Liberal was founded back in 1880 to promote liberal thought and religion was forbidden. In fact it was advertised as a town for free thinkers. But it would allow, "No priests, preachers, saloon, God or Hell." Eventually some Christians moved in and they were separated with a barbed wire fence. The "free thinkers" were really open only to thoughts that agreed with their own preconceived ideas! Of course that was before the founder became a devout Christian.

The conductor of the Washington University Glee Club had earlier been in trouble for his group's singing. On November 21, 1895, the conductor was forced to resign after the faculty criticized a song he had written. The song ended with the words, "If you want a kiss, why take it." The university felt it unseemly to sing of "human passion." So you couldn't sing about love and you couldn't sing about God. Time to just play the accordion – that couldn't offend anyone!

Just Spell My Name Right.

Having good public relations is important for government agencies. So on May 15, 1913, when a large number of federal marshals left Springfield for the wilds of Ripley and Oregon counties to break up some illicit stills, they issued a press release. These stills in the hills were important because they were said to be the last in Missouri. The press releases, however, got out before the raids and the shiners knew the marshals were coming. Of course the whole thing failed.

St. Louis Zoo

This free zoo is a wonderful place and recognized as one of the best in the world but there have been a number of questionable decisions made along the way in its proud history. A few of them follow here.

Whadya-mean More Jobs?

On December 2, 1913, St. Louis Mayor Kiel signed an ordinance establishing a zoo in St. Louis in Forest Park. The idea was almost killed because of a lawn-mowing dispute. The guys who mowed the city's property somehow couldn't understand that developing the second largest urban park in America might mean job security and plenty of work.

You Named Her What?

On April 5, 1916, the St. Louis Zoo was officially dedicated and the elephant arrived to lead a parade of 3000 school children. School had children raised money to bring an elephant to the St. Louis Zoo. It was to be named for the Board of Education president, James Harper. It turned out however that the pachyderm was a female so her name was bestowed as "Miss Jim".

Chimps in Rush Hour

On April 13, 1934, it was announced that chimps at the St. Louis Zoo were learning a new show and were being taught signals and signs for driving small cars. The zoo considered a publicity stunt of having the chimps get actual drivers licenses.

Who Bought this Bird?

Newspapers were reporting on November 11, 1930 that the new parrot at the St. Louis Zoo was cursing visitors and telling them to go to Hell. He would be removed from display.

Who Stole the Chimp?

The chimp, Mr. Moke, was kidnapped from the St. Louis Zoo on December 21, 1959. The chimpnapper was hoping to take the bright primate to Hollywood and get rich. The villain found that Mr. Moke was too famous and he was never able to profit from his mistake in judgement.

A Rookie Mistake

It was August 7, 1915 and Miller Huggins, the Cardinals Manager was coaching third base with runners on when the Brooklyn Trolley Dodgers sent a rookie pitcher to the mound. Huggins said he wanted to examine the baseball and the rookie tossed it to him. The runner on third then scored.

Daring Young Men in Flying Machines

On August 1, 1943, an "all St. Louis-built glider" crashed, killing all ten on board, including civic leaders and the president of Robertson Aircraft Corporation. 5000 spectators saw it all.

Truman Never Had a Chance!

By now it's famous. Do you remember the picture from November 3, 1948? At the St. Louis Union Station, Harry Truman displayed the famous newspaper headline, "Dewey Defeats Truman." The papers made a big mistake!

The Perfect Building for the Job

Everyone was delighted on October 19, 1955 when the *Globe-Democrat* reported on the new Military Personnel Records Center in St. Louis. The Commander said the building was constructed in such a way that water used to fight any fire would not harm the vital records. The new building to hold military records for all years and all services was dedicated in Overland, MO on April 17, 1956. It was one of the 20 largest buildings in the world. Of course it was designed to be fireproof.

Then, on July 12, 1973, a night-shift maintenance employee left a cigarette burning on the top floor. The result – this building, as large as 28 football fields, burned for 50 hours and most of the paper records were lost to fire or water.

Military Personnel Records Center – St. Louis

Knowing Your Limitations

On March 12, 1956, a developer approached the County Council in Clayton with a plan for building the world's tallest building there. It was to be 120 stories tall. Clayton had a limit at that time of five stories. How different things might have been in the entire metropolitan area if they had put up that building!

For comparison, remember that for a time the Mercantile Building in St. Louis was the tallest building in Missouri. Then in July of 1980, Kansas City got the 42-story Hyatt Regency. Then St. Louis got the 44-story Southwestern Bell Building.

Just Another No-Talent Bum

It was October 21-23, 1955, and an unknown singer was the opening act for Roy Acuff's three days in St. Louis. No one seemed excited about the unknown singer, Elvis Presley. In fact it was even worse than unexcited when the August 27, 1956 edition of the *Globe-Democrat* a columnist wrote that Elvis Presley, "...cannot sing and his performance is crude and disgusting...his face is devoid of expression except for when he snarls. My guess is that in a comparatively short time he will be forgotten. We can be fairly certain that the King of Rock & Roll didn't worry too much about the no-talent bum at the *Globe-Democrat*.

The Vandeventer Overpass

After seven years of detours, traffic jams, and headaches during construction, the Vandeventer overpass on Highway 40 opened in St. Louis on June 27, 1957. Soon the new roadway was recognized as the "world's longest parking lot."

Never-Never Land

On May 20, 1963, Walt Disney was touring the Riverfront in St. Louis as people talked of a project called Riverfront Square. By March 16, 1964, Disney had announced plans to open an entertainment complex back in his home state. (on the St. Louis Riverfront) Gussie Busch insisted that he sell beer there but Disney said no. It was reported that Auggie Busch "loudly insulted" Walt Disney because Disney wouldn't sell beer in his proposed new park. A short time later Disney announced plans for a complex in Orlando.

The Birds

Gov. Hearnes had complained about the starlings at the Governor's Mansion. So on August 21, 1967, five men shot and killed 2000 birds on and around the Mansion Grounds. It turned out that the birds were not starlings at all but purple martins, a valuable species protected by state and federal law. Oops!

Just Do It!

A plan was announced on May 18, 1966 to shine some lights on the Gateway Arch. The project was completed thirty-five years later. On September 11, 2013, the lights were turned off in memory of the Twin Towers attack. When they tried to turn them back on, the lights stayed dark. They just barely got them back on in time for the October 23 opening game of the World Series.

Congratulations Sweetheart

On May 7, 1974, the Gateway Arch welcomed its five-millionth visitor. It was a nine-year-old girl from Illinois. Among her special attendance prizes were a case of wine and some tickets to the St. Louis Playboy Club.

No One Will Be Interested.

It was May 27, 1977, and a fun little movie called *Star Wars* opened in just one St. Louis theater. (The Creve Coeur Cine) Theater owners didn't think many people would want to see a movie about space and androids.

Whodathunkit?

It was a big day on November 9, 1980 when the valves were opened to flood the new reflecting pools at the Gateway Arch. But after a month, no one could figure out why the pools wouldn't hold water. Then they got it – they had left four drains open.

Risky Business

Kenneth Swyers of Overland made his big mistake on November 22, 1980. He decided to parachute to the top of the Gateway Arch as a publicity stunt. He did just that, but the wind continued to blow after he landed. It pulled his chute, tangled his lines and he rolled and slid down the north leg of the Arch to his death.

One daredevil had better luck with his stunt. On September 14, 1992, John Vincent scaled the Gateway Arch using suction cups. He then BASE jumped from the top.

Don't Jump!

Suicide is always a bad decision but it can be an especially bad one. On May 11, 1979, a man jumped off the McCutcheon overpass on Hwy. 40 in St. Louis. He bounced off a van and landed in the eastbound lanes. And yes, he survived.

Fill It Up with Regular, Mack.

On January 9, 1984, a DC-3 cargo plane crashed in Bridgeton only a few feet from Interstate 70 and a residential subdivision. An airport worker had put jet fuel into the propeller-driven plane.

Don't Take Advice from Idiots.

Schools and businesses closed while families stocked up on supplies. December 3, 1990 was predicted to see a gigantic earthquake along the New Madrid Fault. Nothing happened. This writer was teaching at a school that decided to stay open on that day. However, they prepared an earthquake evacuation plan which left the students and teachers assembled in a nearby park. It was a good idea, except that they seemed to forget that the park was immediately below the dam of the city's largest lake. Not a good place to be during an earthquake!

When You're in the Public Eye . . .

A prostitution sting operation at a St. Louis airport hotel on March 10, 1991 turned up a surprise – the St. Louis Prosecuting Attorney, George Peach. Oops!

How'd That Get There?

It was a sad day for State Treasurer, Wendell Bailey on November 12, 1991 when he tried to take a handgun on an airliner. To make matters even worse, it was later determined that the gun's serial numbers had been altered. Two bad decisions, Mr. Bailey!

If You Can Read This . . .

Nostradamus, the Mayan calendar, and others predicted that on December 21, 2012 the world would end. Congratulations if you are reading this book.

Missouri's Scariest . . .

SCARIEST JOBS:

Farmer

It's obvious that farming can be very dangerous because of things like large animals, powerful equipment, and chemicals. However, on June 5, 1913 the _Elsberry Democrat_ told of a different kind of danger for one of their farmers who was just plowing his field. John R. Hutts, of near Mokane, was attacked by several colonies of bees. The man was unconscious when neighbors rushed in and carried him from the vicinity and nearly 200 stingers were extracted from his head and face. One of his horses was ruined and the other killed by the bees.

Amusement Park Worker

At least it would have been scary to work at the pier at Winnwood Amusement Park in Kansas City. Back on July 5, 1935, the pier collapsed sending people falling two stories into the mud below. Joining them were a box full of snakes which had been on exhibit. Over fifty people were injured including some with snakebites. Sure, it would have been scary to fall into the water with those snakes but it would also be scary to get out of the water into the crowd of victims. I'll bet they were upset with the park and it's employees!

It would have also been a frightening job on July 25, 1978 when a gondola fell from the Skyway ride at Six Flags in Eureka. Three young people were killed and one seriously injured. Many more were stranded 200 feet in the air as a thunderstorm approached. So picture yourself 200 feet in the air with lightning striking and you're extracting frightened people from little gondolas swinging on a broken cable.

Nuclear Policeman

On December 15, 1951, the mayor of St. Louis approved plans to appoint 5,000 auxiliary police officers to help in the event of nuclear attack. Their jobs would be to patrol devastated areas. Would you volunteer to patrol areas devastated by nuclear explosions? It sounds like the beginning of a really scary movie.

Zoo Keeper

I wouldn't have wanted to go to work at the Reptile House in the St. Louis Zoo. Back on August 28, 1970, a zoo-keeper left a drain open and a deadly king cobra escaped. They went ahead and opened the reptile house to the public because they were sure that cobras were nocturnal. Forty days later the snake was found and put back into his cage. I might have called in sick for 40 days.

Dickerson Park Zoo in Springfield was a dangerous place to work on October 11, 2013. A female elephant who seemed to be upset by the death of another elephant attacked and killed her keeper.

Road Repair Worker

Repairing county roads doesn't seem like such a frightening job, does it? A repair crew working near Sullivan might feel differently. On July 29, 2013, Franklin County workers repairing a road near Sullivan found a problem. Water had washed away a big pocket of soil and now it was filled with hundreds upon hundreds of snakes. Of course they had to go on and make the repairs. Would that be considered a hostile work environment?

SCARIEST MOVIES:

The St. Louis Death Reel

On November 10, 1912, *The Post-Dispatch* reported on something known as the "St. Louis Death Reel." Albert Bond Lambert had a motion picture film of aviation pioneers taken at an air meet at Kinloch Field earlier in the year. Seven of the people on the film had since died. Another, Teddy Roosevelt, had been recently shot and wounded in an assassination attempt. Say "cheese." (and goodbye)

The Exorcist

After a long deliberation, Catholic Church officials gave a qualified nod of approval of the new movie, *The Exorcist* on January 13, 1974. It was possibly the scariest movie of all time and some people don't know that it was based on a true story. Since the movie version showed it all happening on and near the Georgetown University campus many folks don't realize that it was actually based on an incident in St. Louis, near St. Louis University.

SCARY EVENTS:

What Could it Be?

On August 20, 1870, an unsolved mystery developed at Rush Tower (Herculaneum). Pretty young Miss Weaver had a party at her father's home then went to bed. She was found in the morning on her back with her arms folded across her chest and dead. The *New York Herald* reported, "Preparations were made for burial, but before the body could be placed in the coffin the corpse began to swell, and great quantities of blood poured from the mouth, nose and ears. It could not be staunched, and with difficulty was kept from saturating everything around the body. The features became distended, and the color of the body black, the whole change occurring within a short time after the discovery." This event remains unique and unsolved.

SCARY FUN:

Outlaw Run is a roller coaster at Silver Dollar City in Branson. In 2013 it officially gained <u>three</u> World Records!

 1. Its double barrel-roll makes it the only roller coaster in the world to take riders upside-down.

 2. Its 162 foot drop at 81° is the steepest drop for any wood coaster in the world.

 3. Its outside-banked turn is the first on any wood roller coaster in the world.

Just for good measure, its top speed of 68 mph makes it the fastest in Missouri and the second-fastest in the world. That's the best kind of scary!

SCARIEST PLACES:

If I would have to choose the scariest place ever in Missouri, I would probably say the Alexian Brothers Hospital in St. Louis where the child was taken in the event known in books and movies as the most famous exorcism. (This was mentioned previously in the "Scariest Movies" section.) But that hospital no longer exists so this writer's present pick as the scariest place in the state is The Screaming House in Union, Missouri.

Many Bizzare and unexplained events have taken place there for as long as anyone can remember. Kids can read more about them in *Mysterious Missouri* by Ross Malone and adults can read even more in *The Screaming House* which was written by Steven A. LaChance. Steven actually lived in the house for a time before being driven out in the middle of the night.

Missouri's Strangest

STRANGEST PEOPLE:

Our Strangest Governor

Our 14th Governor, Robert M. Stewart was born on March 12, 1815. It is said that he rode his horse into the Governor's Mansion and fed it oats from the furniture. He was also famous for being on his "toots" with alcohol and sometimes hard to find. His main political skill was an ability to come down on both sides of any argument.

Dr. McDowell

Dr. Joseph McDowell was born on April Fool's Day if 1805. He was very much respected as a surgeon and teacher but he had a dark side. He did bizarre experiments on cadavers and was accused of grave-robbing. He is known to have experimented on dead family members and to have sealed his son's and daughter's bodies inside a cave in Hannibal. With these two bodies hanging inside the cave, local boys like Sam Clemens loved to explore what later became known as Mark Twain's Cave. He writes of this cave in *The Adventures of Tom Sawyer*. Do you remember that Clemens also wrote of grave robbers at work in Hannibal?

Then people began to learn of Dr. McDowell's activities after some boys playing a ball game found dissected bodies outside the St. Louis University Medical School. Soon mobs formed and attacked the school. McDowell fought back and, at one point, got a bear from his museum and sent the animal to attack the crowd. The school was eventually destroyed and the mobs roamed the city looking for targets at other medical schools. At one school the students hid the bodies and the crowd went away disappointed. Newspapers said that by February 29, 1844, things were getting back to normal in the city.

Prove It!

The newspapers tell us that on May 17, 1890, a Mr. Blumenstengel was declared insane by the County Court. Well, how do you know he was crazy? As evidence, one doctor pointed out the fact that Mr. Blumenstengel had run for Mayor of De Soto. I suppose that proves it.

A Truly Plucky Girl

The editor of the *Hillboro Democrat* newspaper was truly impressed on July 16, 1891 when he bragged, "Hillsboro has the pluckiest little girl in the state we believe. Constable Forrest's 10-year-old girl caught a rat with her bare hands that just one day last week, had caught a small chicken. The girl is a trump, and we are proud of her."

Aunt Phoebe

Back in February of 1912, a mysterious prowler was wandering through Mountain Grove. Described as a man wearing a long overcoat and a woman's hat, locals called him "Aunt Phoebe."

STRANGE HAPPENINGS:

The Worst Wedding Reception

Henry Fry and Rebecca Baker, along with some friends were headed for Ste. Genevieve on the first of March, 1797 when they were jumped by Indians. The Indians took the wedding guest's clothes and took the food from the wagon. This food was for the wedding feast. The wedding was postponed for one year.

A Good Prank

Imagine the scene: It was June 3, 1812, a terrible storm was followed by a dense fog and a downtown St. Louis church bell began ringing with no one touching the rope. Residents fell to their knees. What could it mean? When the fog lifted they saw a rope running from the bell to another church belfry across the street.

Dueling

Some things that seem strange to us today were all too common in the past. One of those things was dueling. On September 4, 1813, Andrew Jackson and Thomas Hart Benton had a shootout followed by a knife fight in a Tennessee hotel's hallway on this date. This caused Benton to leave Tennessee and move to Missouri. Later Benton went to the US Senate from Missouri and Jackson was elected from Tennessee. The only available desks forced them to sit side-by-side in the Senate Chamber.

The Disappearing Delegate

On October 2, 1820 in the "State Capital Building", which was the Missouri Hotel in St. Louis, Missouri's first two US Senators were selected. (David Barton and Thomas Hart Benton) The deciding vote was cast by Daniel Ralls from Pike County and for whom Ralls County is named. He was so ill on October 2nd that he had to be carried, still in his bed, to the meeting of the Legislature. He died four days later. Hearing of his father's death, a son came to St. Louis to claim the body but no body or burial place could be found.

Strangest War

Missouri has endured many wars within her borders and beyond. Of course we know of the War Between the States and the Missouri-Kansas Border War. There was also the Heatherly War, the Mormon War, and the terrible Slickers War. Strangest of all was the Honey War. On December 12, 1839, the Missouri and Iowa Militias were squared off for battle in The Honey War when a last-minute truce averted bloodshed. The militias were brought for battle because of a dispute over a honey tree near the border.

These militia men were not soldiers and they had no uniforms. Many didn't even have guns. One man came armed with only a sausage grinder. We suppose that could be pretty intimidating. This was December and it's cold along the Iowa border but some didn't even have blankets or tents. But those from Pike County did have 5 wagon-loads of whiskey. Some of the Iowa men mispronounced "Pike" and yelled insults about Puke County. That is why, for a time, Missouri's nickname was the Puke State. Don't expect to see that on any license plates.

Don't Make a Pig of Yourself.

After years of Civil War, good food was sometimes hard to find. Especially beef and pork. On September 4, 1865, Springfield newspapers were reporting that, "owing to the fondness of the soldiers for fresh pork, when they were here, there was a great scarcity of stock horses in the county, and these animals were very dear." Yes, it was quoted correctly. They only thought it was pork.

By 1875, pork was in plentiful supply but on November 23 it was reported that New Yorkers in Kansas City hotels were hoping to eat some buffalo meat. One hotel restaurant served them roast pork and, thinking it was buffalo, they went away happy.

Ancient Aliens?

It was way back on October 19, 1865 when the *Missouri Democrat* newspaper reported that a trapper, James Lumley, had seen a "bright luminous body" in the skies moving toward the east. Then, there was a loud explosion and the smell of sulphur in the air. He found the large object which was divided into compartments and had something like hieroglyphs on its surface. He also discovered glass & "strange stains."

Strange Counties

Of course you know that St. Louis broke away from St. Louis County and now they are separate political entities. The city of St. Louis is actually its own county. Two other counties also deserve notice because of their strange political past.

The Civil War was heating up on October 17, 1861 when Colonel Jefferson Jones formed a force of Callaway County residents to resist the Union forces and sent the federals a proposal. If they withdrew, he would disband his forces, and the county would be loyal to neither the Confederacy nor the Union. He had made his county an area outside of any government control. That is why, even today, it is called the "Kingdom of Callaway."

Then, one hundred years later someone in Jefferson City made a mistake. They left McDonald County off the state's official tourism map. The little county in Southwest Missouri depends heavily on tourism for economic growth. So on April 6, 1961 McDonald County called their representatives home from Jefferson City, seceded from the state, and formed McDonald Territory. This publicity stunt saw the county form a militia, issue visas and sell territorial postage stamps. The end result was that they got lots of good natured recognition and the tourist economy boomed.

The Capital in St. Louis

It is common today to hear people say that the politicians get to Washington D.C. and forget all about us. They call it the "Inside the Beltway Mentality." But this isn't anything new. A century-and-a-half ago people were also feeling that the people in Washington were out of touch. On October 20, 1869 the people held The National Capital Removal Convention in St. Louis to discuss the possibilities of moving the national capital to a city in the Mississippi Valley.

Then fourteen months later, the *St. Louis Globe-Democrat* reported that a large movement was underway to move the nation's capital to St. Louis. Supporters said Washington was too far away and out of touch with the rest of America. Finally on October 29, 1877, at a special session of Congress a bill was introduced on this date to move the nation's capital to St. Louis.

Of course you know that the national capital city is still Washington, D. C. but the story of St. Louis as a capital city was not quite over. On December 8, 1948, St. Louis officials left for London with a pitch to make Missouri the "World Capital" as people were considering the idea of a United Nations organization. The U.N. facilities would have been located at Weldon Spring in St. Charles County.

What Town Is This?

A newspaper printed on June 4, 1871, told of the first passenger train that arrived at the new town which had yet to find a name. The newspaper reported, "Bewildered passengers got off the train, mentally measuring the town consisting of no more than three structures." The town is now named Vandalia. If they asked, "Where are we?" no one knew.

Strangest Ferry Boat

On December 12, 1873, merchants in St. Louis organized a ferry service at Third and Washington where the mud flowed "deepest and most rapid." Shoppers and merchants would step aboard the ferry boat and be pulled across the street by ropes.

We'll Make You Sick & Then We'll Cure You.

The *Carthage Banner* reported on May 28, 1874 that two men captured a rattlesnake six feet, seven inches long with 27 rattles and, to them, it looked like a business opportunity. You see, in Cassville whiskey could only be used for medical purposes and it was also known as a cure for snakebite. The two men mentioned above were offering to let the snake bite any man for 15 cents and they would throw in one drink of medicine.

A Joke on a Joker

News reached Missouri on June 16, 1875 that Mark Twain was in trouble. When a boy stole his umbrella he offered a $205.00 reward. $5.00 was for the umbrella and $200.00 for "the boy's remains." He was arrested when a corpse turned up at his home along with a note claiming the reward. (Some jokers at a local medical college had sent a corpse.)

Another Good Joke

Some boys in St. Louis knew how to startle people back on August 11, 1872. An astronomer had predicted that a comet was coming and would hit St. Louis. Many people panicked and many left town. Young boys added to the problems by standing on street corners and occasionally yelling, "Here she comes!"

Stay Out of the Water!

Several noted scientists expressed interest in recent reports of a "sea serpent" sighted in the Mississippi River at eastern Missouri on August 19, 1877. It was described as 30-feet-long with dark scales, a head like a dog, and a mouth like a pelican.

Big Doin's in Buffalo

The big news around Buffalo, MO on June 11, 1885, was the removal from a local lady of a ninety pound tumor!

Promises, Promises,

The Festus newspaper correspondent known only as "Damphool" was reporting on April 17, 1890 that another magician was in town. The fellow promised to cut off his own head and lay it on a platter before the audience.

Champion Rat Hunter

The *Audrain County Republican* reported on November 17, 1876 that Mr. David Crockett of Audrain County killed 341 rats in his corn cribs. That's very interesting but why did he wait so long? How could he have allowed 341 rats to be living in his harvested corn?

Champion Squirrel Hunters

A local newspaper reported back on March 27, 1890, that schoolboy, Charles Schubert of Rock Creek was such a good squirrel hunter that one squirrel "gave himself up" by entering the Schubert home and waiting on the rafters for the boy to come home from school and shoot him. His parents must have been so proud of how their son could shoot squirrels inside their home!

The next year, that paper reported that Squirrels were overrunning Jefferson County and people were serious about cutting their numbers. On one Friday afternoon and Saturday a small group of men from Hillsboro shot 58 of them.

Drunken Pigeon Hunters?

No, not drunken hunters – drunken pigeons! On January 25, 1959, the St. Louis Health and Hospital Director announced a plan to get swarms of pigeons drunk on alcohol-soaked bread crumbs. The drunken birds would then be scooped up and hauled off to the city pound's gas chamber. Bird lovers killed the plan instead of the birds.

Strange Times at School and (Marjorie Allen & Carl Fisher)

We already reported that Springfield set a record as being the largest school district in the state and some other records will follow on later pages. But here are some other things to ponder about schools in the state.

On September 6, 1867, an important school election was taking place in Rock Port. The opposition to the issue said they were, "Opposed to education, civilization and railroads." Further they were, "Opposed to building school houses in Clay Township, Atchison County or anywhere in the state." So, when you're opposed to building a school house anywhere in the state and to civilization in general, where do you go from there?

Some people were opposed to having married teachers, women teachers, male teachers, divorced teachers, or teachers who were known to be "courting." Others were opposed to teachers who did such scandalous things as visiting a barber shop or playing baseball. And then there is the matter of teachers' pay. On July 19, 1913 – The *Mountain Grove Journal* reported on an old teacher, H. L. Mabrey of Wayne County, had the copy of a contract he made to teach in that county in 1848. "The yearly salary was $15 and the teacher agreed to accept "cash, port, beef hides, deer skins, raccoon skins, or any fur if good, also woolen jeans cloth, shirting cloth or young cattle not over one year old, young beef steer or cow".

Strange Times at School and (Marjorie Allen & Carl Fisher) (Continued)

On May 8, 1913, the mayor of Springfield got a bright idea. He would use the school children as salesmen and eradicate the houseflies of the city. He ordered 3,000 fly swatters for sale to school children at 3 cents each. The children were then instructed to peddle them around town for 5 cents each and see that every house was supplied.

Marjorie Allen

In spite of all that and much more the communities continued to find good teachers and one of those actually set a record as she did her job. On September 14, 2011, Marjorie Allen was recognized for 72 years of excellent teaching in the Normandy School District! She was still working in the district as a substitute teacher at that time.

Carl Fisher

Carl Fisher from Pleasant Hope, Missouri holds another very special record. He was recognized on November 19, 2012 as a World Record holder for running up the planet's longest career as a bus driver. He drove a rural Missouri school bus for 66 years! He must have nerves of steel!

Strange Dentist

On July 10, 1891, J. C. Lee was released from custody and left town. He had been pretending to be a dentist. He set up a practice in Hillsboro with borrowed tools and no training.

The Strangest Bird

A doctor Red from Richwoods, was in DeSoto studying "birdology." The October 17, 1891, newspaper reports said that City Drug Store had what seemed to be "a cross between an eagle and an owl, or something else."

Strange Times at the Fair!

There were always exciting things happening at the St. Louis World's Fair but there were plenty of strange things happening also. Since it took a long time to build and organize the Fair, workers were living their lives at the locations for a good time prior to 1904.

On August 20, 1902, the first birth and the first death occurred on the World's Fair Grounds on the same day. Louisiana Purchase O'Leary was born to Mr. and Mrs. Larry O'Leary. The baby lived for nearly a hundred years. Her father was a construction worker at the Fair. A few hours later a rigger, Alfred Willis died when a sledgehammer fell 75 feet and struck him on the head. It was also strange that the Fair (real name, Louisiana Purchase Exposition) was supposed to begin in the spring of 1903 – one hundred years after the Purchase. Because of delays, it actually opened a year late but no one seemed to mind. Finally with a speech from the President, music by the Marine Corps Band, tens of thousands of people attended the grand opening day.

Strange Times at the Fair! (Continued)

Some of the most interesting events started on March 25, 1904 when the most popular and famous people at the World's Fair arrived by train. They were the dog-eating, head-hunting, "wild people" from the Philippines. More correctly they were known as the Irrogate People. Four days after their arrival, they shocked the local populace when they asked their contact man for a favor. So, on this day, he requested that the master of the dog pound supply eight dogs per day to the Irrogates – for their meals.

On April 4, the Women's Humane Society heard the results of an investigation which showed that the Igorote people who were eating dogs at the World's Fair killed the dogs by beating them to death. The women suggested that the Igorates be supplied with canned dog meat which was readily available. Does it surprise you that canned dog meat was readily available in St. Louis at that time?

Strange Times at the Fair! (Continued)

On the 6th of April, Professor Frederick Starr brought a group of people from the Island of Yezzo (Hokkaido, Japan) who were described as "very dark in color and generally untidy" to the World's Fair. Starr billed the bearded men and tattooed women as "the hairiest people on earth.

Inflation was becoming a problem at the World's Fair by April 10. Governor Hunt of the Philippine Village complained that he was paying $2.00 for dogs that normally wouldn't bring ten cents. Think about that for a minute! There is a familiar old story that the Dogtown neighborhood in St. Louis got its name because the Irrogate people used to sneak over there at night and take dogs. Actually the Dogtown name is much older than the World's Fair.

On the 14th of April, Seven Teheulche Indians arrived at the World's Fair from Patagonia. They demanded, and got, a diet of horsemeat. It was becoming less safe to be a pet or livestock in the area.

April 19, 1904 was a big day at the fair. A baby girl was born in the Philippine Village. A girl as your first baby was considered bad luck so the infant was ignored by the parents and she died a few days later. It was truly upsetting many Americans to learn about the lifestyles of other people firsthand

It was an exciting day on June 5, when 8000 people paid to see a bull fight at the Arena. The Sheriff stopped the show and the angry crowd burned the building to the ground. The show's promoter put on a disguise and skipped town with the receipts. That left the matador and the understudy arguing over money. On June 8 the later killed the former. What fun!

Strange Times at the Fair! (Continued)

Things hadn't settled down much by the 18th. That was when members of the cast of a Wild West show got into an actual shootout. One cowboy was wounded and one bystander was killed.

Then, on June 24, the War Department stepped in and ordered the primitive people at the World's Fair to wear more clothing. (Yes, the War Department. We know it doesn't make sense but it's true.) We invited them here so we could learn about their culture then we insist that they dress more like us.

A group of African pygmies arrived at the Fair on June 30. Ota Benga became the best known of the group and, after the fair, he was offered an opportunity to stay in the U.S. and was promised free food and housing. He liked life at the Fair and this sounded like a good deal so he agreed. That's how it happened that after the Fair he was taken to New York and put on display in the monkey house at the Bronx zoo. He shot himself in 1916.

The Humane Society was back making news at the fair on August 14. Society officials tried to arrest cowboys and Indians at the World's Fair for roping and tying cattle. The cowboys and Indians attacked the officers and the fans joined in when the show was temporarily canceled.

Speaking of Indians, it was August 15 when 76-year-old Geronimo showed up at the arena and was roping calves. He did very well and got a good round of applause from the audience. He arrived so late at the Fair because he was holding out for more money. He won his negotiations and finally arrived. He was a real showman and did well with the crowd. It's also interesting however that this man, one of the bravest of all men, didn't like the huge Ferris wheel and wanted no part of it.

Strange Times at the Fair! (Continued)

The *St. Louis Globe* reported on November 5 that the pygmies living in the International Village at the Fair saw an airship (balloon) and wanted to buy one. They were convinced it would make them great elephant hunters. They asked one official to negotiate for them and promised the first set of tusks as payment. (Doesn't this sound like the beginning of a Woody Allen movie?)

The very next day Immigration officials were looking into rumors that the Chinese who were "on exhibit" at the World's Fair were gathering weapons. It was reported that there had already been several escape attempts and that they might refuse to go home.

Missouri's biggest party came to an end on December 1, 1904 when David Francis said, "Farewell to all thy splendor." and threw a switch closing the World's Fair.

A Strange Farm

The *Cassville Republican* reported on December 22, 1910 that hopes ran high for a Barry County man who was establishing a skunk farm near Madry, MO. We wondered why anyone would operate a skunk farm. It turns out that many people used to think skunks were good pets. There is still at least one very modern skunk farm raising de-scented pets for sale. In 1910, skunks were also sold to farmers for ridding their grain cribs of vermin. Skunk pelts were popularly sold as "American sable," and the carcasses were boiled into a tallow used for waterproofing boots and shoes. You can read more about this in *The Monett Nine*.

Strange but True Plane Crash

On March 7, 1911 the new DeChenne Aeroplane was flying above Joplin. Then the rudder wire broke and the plane became unbalanced. As it fell, the pilot climbed out on the rods, wires, and canvas that comprised the plane and balanced the machine as it descended. The pilot, Ed Wilson, escaped with injuries. Wilson's former occupation was as a trapeze artist.

He Did What?

According to the April 4, 1912 *Mountain Grove Journal,* "Sid Collins laid two eggs which weighed nine ounces on the table of the *Lamar Republican-Sentinel* last week." That would really be news if . . .

An Eggsplosion?

On July 25, 1912, it was reported in the *Seymour Citizen* that, "A decayed egg exploded under a hen at Jake Bender's a few days ago and set the chicken house on fire besides tearing the hen into several pieces.

Pride in Our Craftsmanship

It was Halloween day back in 1912, when the *St. Louis Post-Dispatch* reported that the unclaimed body of a man had been standing in the window of a St. Louis mortuary for 27 years. They were displaying him to demonstrate the skill of their embalming.

Another Skunk Farm

The Mountain Grove Journal reported on March 27, 1913 that "the Rippee Bros. opossum and pole cat (skunk) farm had secured several of the animals and prospects for the business were good." This does sound strange to us in modern times but skunks had many uses in 1913 and skunk farming was a good business. Read more about skunk farms in *The Monett Nine.*

Pete Kibble's Foot

Pete Kibble's foot is buried up in Milan, Missouri. Pete was a local guy who lost his foot in a railroad accident. He had the foot buried in Oakwood Cemetery, under a marker that reads, "Pete Kibble's Foot 1917." He did that so he would have a grave available and someday, when the rest of him died, he could be reunited with his foot. But then Pete had a change of heart and went out to the Wild West never to return. As a result, there remains in Milan's Oakwood Cemetery a grave clearly marked as Pete Kibble's Foot. If you travel the world, how many things like that will you see?

You Are My Soul and My Inspiration.

Beginning on July 8, 1913, a fairly uneducated St. Louis woman named Pearl Curran wrote four critically acclaimed books and hundreds of poems about life as a New England Pilgrim. She claimed that it all came to her through her Ouija board from the long dead Pilgrim lady, Patience Worth.

Warning! Warning!

The crowd listened intently on November 4, 1921 when Evangelist Billy Sunday told a crowd at the St. Louis Coliseum, "The world is going to hell so fast you can smell the smoke as old Satan stamps his foot on the accelerator."

Good Bye – Hello

Between games of a double header on May 30, 1922, the Cardinals and Cubs completed a deal. So for the second game, Max Flack and Cliff Heathcote traded uniforms and played for their new teams.

The Mummy of Mount Olive

Back in 1924, a truck farmer named Joseph Marconnot died in his home town of Carondelet, Missouri. Joseph had a strong desire to be remembered after his death so he had made plans for his body when the time came. According to his wishes, he was buried in the manner of the Pharaoh, King Tutankhamun. He also ordered that his body should be dressed in a tuxedo.

The Marconnot Mummy's Marvelous Mausoleum

According to his wishes he was placed in a beautiful new mausoleum at the Mount Olive Cemetery and the mausoleum was to have a glass door so people could stop by and admire the Pharaoh Farmer. The neat thing is that, over the years, lots of people did come by to check him out. He became a popular attraction just the way he had planned.

But other people always think they know what's good for us, don't they? One day some people started worrying about vandalism and other things so they decided to replace the plate glass door with one made of stainless steel. Now, when you visit old Joe, you can no longer see the mummified man – just a plain old everyday door.

Another Mummy Behind Glass

Who would ever think that there could have been another mummy displayed behind glass for the world to admire? Well there was one but this one wasn't there of his own choosing. On Halloween day in 1912, the _St. Louis Post-Dispatch_ newspaper reported that the unclaimed body of a man had been standing in the window of a St. Louis mortuary for 27 years. They were displaying him to demonstrate the skill of their embalming.

A Strange Race

An unusual race began on March 4, 1928. the 84-day footrace called The Bunion Derby ran the entire 3,422 mile length of a new highway – Route 66.

A Strange Restaurant

There have been many strange restaurants in Missouri like the Garbage Can Café near Marshfield or the home of Goober Burgers in Sedalia. There is still a very good barbecue restaurant located in a cave above a river near Richland and Waynesville. But one stands out. On March 13, 1942, Lambert's Café in Sikeston opened for business. It became famous for throwing food.

One busy day the owner, Ray Lambert was passing out dinner rolls but was having trouble getting to all the tables. A customer yelled, "just throw the danged thing!" And he did. People thought it was fun and asked for more. On that day Lambert's became "the home of throwed rolls" and people began to come from all around the globe.

All That Way for Nuthin'

The football Cardinals came to St. Louis on March 13, 1960. Even with some great players, many great moments, and two division championship seasons, they played for decades in St. Louis never winning a playoff game of any kind.

Speaking of all that way for nuthin', on December 10, 1972, Jimmy Hart of the St. Louis Cardinals threw a pass from his own one yard line to Ahmad Rashad who was tackled on the one yard line. A 98 yard play with no score!

MoMo, the Missouri Monster

July 11, 1972 was the first modern reported sighting of MoMo, the Missouri Monster, near Louisiana, MO. Eventually sightings were reported in 29 Missouri counties. The furry, foul-smelling, dog-eating, picnic stealing, monster turned out to be some Pike County boys with a borrowed fake fur coat. They inspired a new frozen custard, a thrill ride at Six Flags, a minor movie, a country-western song, and much more. But it all started on that day when three high school boys scared some girls and stole their picnic lunch.

Where's My Lake?

Residents in Chesterfield began to notice that their 23 acre lake was shrinking on June 7, 2004. Within three days the entire Lake Chesterfield was gone and the 67 "lakeside" homes looked out on a muddy stinky mess.

11-11-11

This has seemed like an unusual date in Missouri. You read earlier that on November 11 in 1911 a savage storm hit the entire state and many people and much livestock was lost as temperatures dropped from the eighties into the teens and lower. This was accompanied by heavy rain, hail, sleet, then snow.

Exactly one hundred years later November 11, 2011, about 125 UFOs were reported over the Kansas City metropolitan area. These orange globes would appear, divide, and fly through the sky over K.C., Independence, Raytown, and Lee's Summit. They were followed on radar and recorded by a television news crew.

Rising Caskets

There was a time in mid-August, 1993, when caskets in Missouri began to rise from the ground and swirl around while people with ropes tried to catch them and return them to their graves. This was not a horror movie but a real event. One town, Hardin, had caskets coming up from 1,576 graves and 150 of them escaped with their contents inside.

People who are old enough will remember these rising caskets as a part of the Great Flood of 1993. The ground became super-saturated and could not keep the air-filled boxes from floating to the top of the flood waters.

Mutilations

Among the strange happenings, livestock mutilations may be the most strange. They have gone on for years and we have been unable to record just how many total mutilations have been reported. On August 7, 1978, another in the series of mutilated cows was found – this time near Elsberry. The ears, eyes, and sex organs had been surgically removed. There was no blood anywhere! No one could find any tracks or footprints at the scene – no evidence of any kind. Usually vultures, coyotes, and other scavengers would be all over dead animals but no scavengers would go near these cows. "Crystallized" rubbery flies were found in trees near the bodies.

Then another farmer found a similar mutilated calf. He made a point to be vigilant the next night and that's when he saw a UFO "as big as the Moon" flying over the same field as where the calf had been found. Eight days later another UFO was seen flying over another farm nearby. It flew in an arc and made no sound at all. It glowed bright red. The next day another mutilated calf was found on that farm. Dead cows were found on three farms on the 17th. On the 18th bright UFOs were reported over Elsberry.

One of the most recent and best-documented events happened on July 19, 2013. In Henry County, the papers and the K.C. TV stations were reporting a third cattle mutilation event this month. Surgery with no blood. As with the others, no clues as to who or how. Over a period of three years these strange mutilations were found in Wentzville, Sedalia, Peculiar, Oak Grove, Blue Springs, Iberia, Dixon, and Buffalo. Three were found near Richland.

More U.F.O.s

You remember the Missouri trapper who found the strange craft which seems to have crashed back in 1865. There have been many more strange things seen since then. Most of the sightings have taken place since July 5, 1947, when UFO sightings were reported over much of the state.

The most bizarre events happened from May 8, to May 22, 1941. A Baptist minister in southeast Missouri claimed that he had been called to bless some dead bodies found in a crashed space ship but he was directed not to tell anyone about what he had seen. Then, upon his death, his family told that he left a detailed description of the craft and its passengers. If you go to Sikeston or Cape Girardeau today, you will find that their newspapers have had sections partially removed for those days. No one can tell you what was supposed to be in those sections. Removing the news has added fuel to earlier claims that a spacecraft with dead aliens had been found between Sikeston and Cape Girardeau.

You also remember the story from just above about the Elsberry mutilations. Every time cattle are found mutilated in this strange unexplained way, UFOs are spotted not too far away. Sure enough, the very next day after the Elsberry event, military personnel and others in the Belton area watched a UFO spend 45 minutes in the air above them. Local air bases followed it on radar. Near Belton in 1978, there were two Air Force bases, a missile launch base, a Naval Air Station, and Kansas City International Airport. People in Belton were accustomed to seeing things in the sky. But, just as it was getting dark on this summer evening, August 8, several military personnel saw a UFO fly over and it stayed in the area for about 45 minutes. The military bases even tracked it on radar. This is not a new phenomenon but has been going on for decades and continues to happen with no explanation.

Alligator Hunting in Kennett

You wouldn't normally think of alligators being a problem in Missouri, but on April 4, 2012, the city of Kennett was attempting an alligator roundup. Two years earlier a traveling salesman sold about fifty gators in the town and the "pets" were growing larger and more dangerous.

Pillories for Men and Women

STRANGE LAWS, CRIMES, & PUNISHMENTS:

Behave or Else!

The pillory and whipping post were established on October 1, 1804 as official forms of punishment in Missouri. The whipping post held a person in place while being lashed with a leather bull whip. The pillory held a person's head and wrists while they endured humiliation or physical pain.

The Bachelor Tax

Missouri imposed a $1.00 "bachelor tax" on unmarried men between 21 and 50 years old. This was on December 20, 1820. That left the men only eleven days to find a lady and get married if they wanted to avoid the tax. Can you imagine New Year's Eve that year?

Avoid Jail Time in Gallatin.

On March 2, 1841, the contract was issued to John Comer in Gallatin for the building of the county's original jail. This "pit jail" was the first of three historic "innovative" jails for that county. Then, on November 15, 1858, Gallatin got its new stone jail. Then, on March 1, 1887, the court in Daviess County ordered the building of the famous rotating "Squirrel Cage Jail" in Gallatin. This eight-sided jail contained eight small wedge-shaped cells which rotated so that only one was adjacent to a door at any one time. This limited the chance for escape but stirred many humane objections.

This type of "Lazy Susan Jail" was very secure but it was a problem if there should ever be a fire. Imagine trying to swivel all of the cell doors into place before the occupants were burned alive. This type of jail was also built for Nodaway County at Maryville and DeKalb County at Maysville.

The rotating 'Squirrel Cage Jail', Gallatin, Missouri

Strange Slaves

We all know that slavery existed for a time in Missouri. But the sale of Jack Bowers on July 29, 1847, points up something that many do not know. Jack Bowers was a white man and he was sold to a stable keeper on that day. In 1847, vagrants could be sold to the highest bidder for periods of six months.

Strange Bail

The court in Barry County had a prisoner who couldn't post bail. So, on March 14, 1878, he got out by leaving his wooden leg with the court.

Breaking Bad

A teacher from Hematite was caught pitching horseshoes on Sunday, March 30, 1890. People were questioning if he might be instructing his pupils to play marbles, cards or baseball on Sunday. Oh the shocking immorality of it

Speed Kills!

On August 3, 1882 St. Louis was considering an ordinance banning those pesky new-fangled bicycle things. They were just too fast to be safe. Later it was automobiles that were considered too fast. So by August 3, 1901 automobile owners were protesting against the eight mile per hour speed limit. They claimed that autos could be safe up to 15 miles per hour.

Things were going downhill when, on April 3, 1904, a group of farmers from St. Louis County organized to protest the failure of the state's nine mph speed limit for automobiles. It was too fast! They were trying to force "drivers and automobiles to respect the skittish horse." Sixteen months later, in an effort to keep up with the "scorchers" who were ignoring the eight mile per hour speed limit, the St. Louis Police Dept. acquired a new chase car, "Skidoodle Wagon Number 2" which could go 50 miles per hour.

Even the police had trouble with the cars being too fast for safety. On August 18, 1906, James Cooney was chasing a speeding motorist through forest park at 35 mph when he hit a tree and was thrown from the car and then he was hit by a second chase car. It sounds just like something from a Keystone Cops movie.

On November 10, 1908, St. Louis County farmers were still on the warpath. Farmers around Manchester, MO warned that they had organized a vigilance committee to punish "automobile scorchers." Further, they warned that they would stretch chains across Manchester Road to snag any vehicle whose driver tried to get away.

Speed Kills! (Continued)

Constable George Bode became the first lawman in a rural area of Missouri (Clayton) to obtain a chase car to catch the scorchers who were speeding through his town. On December 5, 1908, he threatened to mount two repeating rifles on his car if needed!

We were getting thoroughly modern on December 10, 1908 when the St. Louis police showed off their new electric police car. Called the "Speed Buggy," it was manufactured by Studebaker and could actually go 60 mph! Surely that would bring an end to high-speed chases!

Can't Escape the Law

Frank Barton first assaulted the Sheriff and was arrested at Hillsboro. Then he assaulted the Sheriff's daughter to make his escape. But on May 24, 1890, he came back and turned himself in claiming that he was being chased by spooks and couldn't stand the racket any longer.

Rules for Hunks

On April 20, 1875, the St. Louis Police Board approved a "Lady's Platoon." The tallest and best looking police officers could apply to just be "hunks" and help the ladies across the streets. On July 7, 1901, the St. Louis police chief set new rules for his patrolmen in the shopping district. These men, selected for their manly good looks, were told they must wear white gloves and decorate their billy clubs with blue tassels. Their principal duty continued to be to smile and help ladies cross the streets.

Carrie Nation

Carrie Nation was born on November 25, 1846. Nation lived in Belton, on a farm in Cass County, and in Independence. This ax-swinging temperance advocate was famous for smashing saloons. She didn't enforce the laws or anything like that. She tried to have new laws passed but, in the meantime, she and her lady friends just smashed the businesses that she didn't like.

On March 25, 1901, tea-totaler, Carrie Nation got off the train for an hour's break in St. Louis. She was already famous by this time but it was a surprise to her when looking across Market Street, she spied the Carrie Nation Bar. She didn't like the comical name the bar's owner had chosen. She marched across the street, pulled out her axe but then stopped when the owner pointed his pistol at her. Police arrived and put her back on her train.

By the time she next arrived in St. Louis, she had mellowed somewhat. On May 23, 1904 Nation was back in Missouri and said she had "decided to cut out the hatchet business." Instead, she would attack saloons with the Bible – especially at the "devil's carnival." (The World's Fair).

She always created a scene and drew attention to her causes. On April 25, 1907, she was back in St. Louis' Union Station but, true to her word, she did not bring her axe. This time she even stayed in the station. Vendors hid all cigarettes because the last time she was there she took the cigarettes from smoker's mouths and hassled gum-chewers.

Of course, she and her cohorts eventually got the Constitution amended to prohibit the selling of alcoholic beverages.

Swift (and Moving) Justice

Of course it was illegal to drink liquor on a passenger train so on October 2, 1912 when Newton County Sheriff I. H. Collier discovered three men drinking liquor on a train between Joplin and Neosho he arrested them. Prosecuting Attorney Saxton and Justice of the Peace Watson also were passengers on the train so they held the men's trial right there on the moving train. They took the prisoners to the rear coach, where court was held. Upon payment of their $5 fines all were released. They had been arrested, tried and convicted without leaving the train.

The Law & Baseball

It was May 26, 1926 and the Cardinals Hall of Fame first baseman found himself being sued. After a fan's nose was broken by a Jim Bottomley home run the fan sued. In court "Sunny Jim" was forced to admit that he "intentionally hit the ball to create a situation known as a home run." He had to pay the fan $3500.

Their Parents Must Be So Proud!

Panty Raids had gotten out of control at Mizzou and spilled over onto the campuses at Christian and Stevens Colleges. So on May 20, 1952, the Governor mobilized the National Guard for duty in Columbia. Young women were trained to use fire hoses to repel the raiders.

And Now, Even Prouder!

A different kind of problem had developed by March 5, 1974. Streaking was at its height and, on this day, 600 streakers claimed a World Record at the University of Missouri.

I'll Obey This Law.

In a statewide referendum on November 3, 1998, State Statute 578.176 was passed by Missouri's voters making it illegal to wrestle a bear.

A Strange Election

Missouri elected a new Governor on November 7, 1944. The opponents in the race were Phil M. Donnelly and Gene Paul Bradshaw. The two lawyers lived in Lebanon and had offices directly across Madison Street from each other. Donnelly garnered exactly 1,731 votes in his home town while Bradshaw also received exactly 1,731. (Donnelly got more votes statewide.)

Electing Dead Men

We're way too intelligent to elect a corpse to office aren't we? However, on October 16, 2000, the candidate for U.S. Senate, Mel Carnahan, was killed in a plane crash. Though trailing in the polls at that time, Missourians elected the dead ex-governor as their next Senator.

Then on April 7, 2009, residents of Winfield, Mo., gave Harry Stonebraker 90 percent of the vote in a mayoral election on Tuesday, even though he died of a heart attack on March 11. For the second time in recent years, Missourians had elected a dead man to office.

We hope you have enjoyed
the trivia in this
Book of Real Missouri Records.

If so, please check out
the other Missouri-themed books
found on the Author's website at:

www.RossMalone.com .

Made in the USA
Lexington, KY
30 October 2019